W9-CMP-617

Espionage and Intelligence Gathering

Other books in the Current Controversies series:

Espionage and Intelligence Gathering

Louise I. Gerdes, *Book Editor*

Daniel Leone, *President*
Bonnie Szumski, *Publisher*
Scott Barbour, *Managing Editor*
Helen Cothran, *Senior Editor*

CURRENT CONTROVERSIES

GREENHAVEN
PRESS ®

San Diego • Detroit • New York • San Francisco • Cleveland
New Haven, Conn. • Waterville, Maine • London • Munich

THOMSON
GALE

LIBRARY OF CONGRESS CATALOGING-IN-PUBLICATION DATA

Espionage and intelligence gathering / Louise I. Gerdes, book editor.
  p. cm. — (Current controversies)
Includes bibliographical references and index.
ISBN 0-7377-1582-0 (pbk. : alk. paper) — ISBN 0-7377-1581-2 (lib. : alk. paper)
  1. Intelligence service—United States. 2. Espionage—United States.
3. Espionage, American. I. Gerdes, Louise I. II. Series.
JK468.I6E73 2004
327.1273—dc21   2003049017

Printed in the United States of America

Contents

Chapter 2: Should the United States Reform Its Espionage and Intelligence-Gathering Methods?

Yes: The United States Should Reform Its Espionage and Intelligence-Gathering Methods

No: The United States Should Not Reform Its Espionage and Intelligence-Gathering Methods

Chapter 3: Do Espionage and Intelligence-Gathering Activities Violate Civil Liberties?

ists who threaten the principle of ordered liberty, some restrictions on civil liberties—such as monitoring digital communications and detaining suspected terrorists—are essential.

Chapter 4: What Challenges Will the Espionage and Intelligence-Gathering Community Face in the Twenty-First Century?

crack computer codes in order to access highly sensitive commercial information and could possibly disrupt the essential functions of large cities.

Foreword

By definition, controversies are "discussions of questions in which opposing opinions clash" (Webster's Twentieth Century Dictionary Unabridged). Few would deny that controversies are a pervasive part of the human condition and exist on virtually every level of human enterprise. Controversies transpire between individuals and among groups, within nations and between nations. Controversies supply the grist necessary for progress by providing challenges and challengers to the status quo. They also create atmospheres where strife and warfare can flourish. A world without controversies would be a peaceful world; but it also would be, by and large, static and prosaic.

The Series' Purpose

The purpose of the Current Controversies series is to explore many of the social, political, and economic controversies dominating the national and international scenes today. Titles selected for inclusion in the series are highly focused and specific. For example, from the larger category of criminal justice, Current Controversies deals with specific topics such as police brutality, gun control, white collar crime, and others. The debates in Current Controversies also are presented in a useful, timeless fashion. Articles and book excerpts included in each title are selected if they contribute valuable, long-range ideas to the overall debate. And wherever possible, current information is enhanced with historical documents and other relevant materials. Thus, while individual titles are current in focus, every effort is made to ensure that they will not become quickly outdated. Books in the Current Controversies series will remain important resources for librarians, teachers, and students for many years.

In addition to keeping the titles focused and specific, great care is taken in the editorial format of each book in the series. Book introductions and chapter prefaces are offered to provide background material for readers. Chapters are organized around several key questions that are answered with diverse opinions representing all points on the political spectrum. Materials in each chapter include opinions in which authors clearly disagree as well as alternative opinions in which authors may agree on a broader issue but disagree on the possible solutions. In this way, the content of each volume in Current Controversies mirrors the mosaic of opinions encountered in society. Readers will quickly realize that there are many viable answers to these complex issues. By questioning each author's conclusions, students and casual readers can begin to develop the critical thinking skills so important to evaluating opinionated material.

Current Controversies is also ideal for controlled research. Each anthology in the series is composed of primary sources taken from a wide gamut of informational categories including periodicals, newspapers, books, United States and foreign government documents, and the publications of private and public organizations. Readers will find factual support for reports, debates, and research papers covering all areas of important issues. In addition, an annotated table of contents, an index, a book and periodical bibliography, and a list of organizations to contact are included in each book to expedite further research.

Perhaps more than ever before in history, people are confronted with diverse and contradictory information. During the Persian Gulf War, for example, the public was not only treated to minute-to-minute coverage of the war, it was also inundated with critiques of the coverage and countless analyses of the factors motivating U.S. involvement. Being able to sort through the plethora of opinions accompanying today's major issues, and to draw one's own conclusions, can be a complicated and frustrating struggle. It is the editors' hope that Current Controversies will help readers with this struggle.

Greenhaven Press anthologies primarily consist of previously published material taken from a variety of sources, including periodicals, books, scholarly journals, newspapers, government documents, and position papers from private and public organizations. These original sources are often edited for length and to ensure their accessibility for a young adult audience. The anthology editors also change the original titles of these works in order to clearly present the main thesis of each viewpoint and to explicitly indicate the opinion presented in the viewpoint. These alterations are made in consideration of both the reading and comprehension levels of a young adult audience. Every effort is made to ensure that Greenhaven Press accurately reflects the original intent of the authors included in this anthology.

"Despite [an] expansive intelligence-gathering system, America has not been invulnerable to attack. Perhaps the best example of the intelligence community's failure to protect Americans is the September 11, 2001, terrorists attacks."

Introduction

From its inception, the United States has engaged in espionage and intelligence-gathering activities in order to defend against its enemies. Intelligence gathering was initially a function of the Department of Defense, which has several agencies under its umbrella: the Defense Intelligence Agency, the intelligence agencies of each arm of the military, the highly secret National Security Agency, the National Reconnaissance Office, and the National Imagery and Mapping Agency. Over the years other executive departments have also created intelligence divisions. The Department of Energy, for example, has an intelligence arm to protect nuclear secrets. The Department of State and the Department of the Treasury also conduct intelligence to safeguard national interests under their protection.

Probably the most well known of the departmental intelligence agencies is the FBI, which is part of the Department of Justice. The FBI was initially a law enforcement agency. Prior to World War II, the Bureau had been winning wide public support for its highly publicized capture of gangsters. With the outbreak of war in Europe in 1939, however, the FBI began to focus more on the investigation of subversion, sabotage, and espionage. After World War II Presidents Harry S. Truman and Dwight D. Eisenhower granted the FBI the authority to conduct background investigations on present and prospective government employees. Many suspected and convicted spies, such as Julius and Ethel Rosenberg, had been federal employees, and FBI background investigations were considered to be vital in cracking major espionage cases. In 1982, following an explosion of terrorist incidents worldwide, FBI Director William Webster made counterterrorism an FBI priority.

Tracking terrorists has always been a priority of the CIA, whose function is to collect and analyze foreign intelligence and distribute it to government officials and other intelligence agencies. The CIA also conducts covert operations to spur changes abroad advantageous to the United States—such as supporting coups to depose uncooperative leaders—while disguising America's role in the action. Although the United States has long been involved in these activities, the CIA itself, as it is presently known, was not established until after World War II came to an end. The agency's origins can be traced directly to that war.

As the United States edged closer to entering the war in Europe, President Franklin D. Roosevelt felt the need for a civilian intelligence agency devoted to national security. In July 1941 he created the office of Coordinator of Information (COI). The agency's primary directive was to monitor the activities of Adolf Hitler. However, only five months later Japan led a surprise attack on Pearl Harbor on December 7, 1941, and the United States declared war against Japan. Since the United States was at war in Europe and in the Pacific, in June 1942 Roosevelt replaced the COI with a more diversified intelligence agency, the Office of Strategic Services (OSS). The OSS developed into a worldwide clandestine service that provided valuable intelligence on enemy targets and directed and analyzed Allied bombing raids. After the war William J. Donovan, head of the OSS, recommended that a civilian-run organization be created to coordinate information gathered by the various military and non-military intelligence communities, and President Harry S. Truman signed the National Security Act of 1947, which established today's CIA. The head of the CIA, the Director of Central Intelligence, also supervises the FBI and the other twelve intelligence agencies that make up the U.S. intelligence community.

Despite this expansive intelligence-gathering system, America has not been invulnerable to attack. Perhaps the best example of the intelligence community's failure to protect Americans is the September 11, 2001, terrorists attacks. On the morning of September 11, nineteen terrorists crashed two planes into the twin towers of the World Trade Center in New York, a third into the Pentagon in Washington, D.C., and a fourth, its actual target unknown, into a rural Pennsylvania field. These attacks killed more than three thousand people. The terrorists responsible for the attacks were believed to be part of al-Qaeda, a network of terrorists under the direction of exiled Saudi millionaire Osama bin Laden. Almost immediately after this tragedy, people began to ask why the nation's vast intelligence community—which had long been monitoring al-Qaeda—failed to prevent the attacks.

Some analysts argue that centralized decision-making at the FBI prevented the bureau from acting on valuable intelligence that could have prevented the attacks. These commentators cite the experiences of FBI agents Ken Williams and Coleen Rowley. In July 2001 agent Williams wrote a memo in which he expressed concern that Osama bin Laden might be sending terrorists to train at U.S. flight schools. Williams recommended canvassing flight schools for people who might be on terrorist watch lists. Although some maintain that William's memorandum essentially predicted the terrorist attacks, FBI headquarters did not act on it. Coleen Rowley revealed that FBI management obstructed the investigation of terrorist suspect Zacarias Moussaoui, who some believe was also involved in the attacks. Rowley and her colleagues were denied permission to search his laptop computer and personal items to uncover evidence of terrorism or terrorist plots.

This centralized decision-making was the result of structural changes made within the FBI in the 1970s in response to criticism about the agency's assaults on civil liberties. FBI documents leaked to the press at that time revealed that the bureau's counterintelligence program, COINTELPRO, had been illegally spying on civil rights, antiwar, and student leaders in a campaign intended to destroy their credibility. In 1976 President Gerald Ford created a commission to investigate intelligence agency abuses and suggest reforms. The Church Commission, led by Senators Frank Church and Otis G. Pike, recommended a more centralized FBI. After implementing the committee's recommendations, the FBI required that agents seek permission from headquarters to pursue investigation of subversives or terrorists. Field agents no longer had the power to begin investigations without evidence that a specific crime had been committed or was going to be committed, and if agents had evidence, they had to wait weeks or months for express approval from headquarters before proceeding. Some analysts claim that these restrictions explain why the FBI failed to utilize the information it had on al-Qaeda to prevent the September 11 terrorist attacks.

Restrictions imposed by President Jimmy Carter also made it difficult for the CIA to gain valuable intelligence on the al-Qaeda terrorists, some claim. During his administration, Carter ordered reforms that called for CIA field officers to obtain approval before recruiting informants with criminal or human rights abuse records. Some experts claim that these restrictions hindered the CIA from obtaining intelligence that could have helped operatives anticipate the terrorist attacks. "These rules make absolutely no sense with respect to terrorist groups because the only people in terrorist groups are people who want to be terrorists," says former CIA director James R. Woolsey. "That means they have a background in violence and human-rights violations."

Other commentators claim that walls between the various intelligence agencies prevented them from sharing important information. According to Dana R. Dillon of the Heritage Foundation, "America's foreign and domestic agencies either do not or cannot share intelligence resources." Jurisdictional obstacles, she argues, discourage sharing. The FBI, as a law enforcement agency, gathers intelligence in order to present it as evidence in court, so it must protect the information to preserve the rights of the accused. The foreign intelligence community, including the CIA, protects its intelligence because it does not want to compromise information or endanger the lives of the informants and agents who provide it. As a result, says Dillon, "a breakdown occurred at the level of interagency communication, allowing two hijackers to board commercial planes despite being on the Central Intelligence Agency's watch list."

Other analysts maintain that fundamental cultural differences have long hindered cooperation between the CIA and FBI. The CIA was established to collect intelligence abroad, and its charter forbids it to conduct investigations inside the United States. Instead, it passes on intelligence relevant to domestic concerns to the FBI, which handles domestic investigations. These analysts assert that the United States often fails to anticipate cross-border threats like terrorism because it lacks a single agency devoted to collecting, analyzing, and piecing together both domestic and foreign information.

Still others argue that restrictions on surveillance prevent intelligence agencies from obtaining essential information on terrorist activities. The Foreign Intelligence Surveillance Court (FICA) is a secretive panel of federal judges that considers requests from the U.S. Intelligence community to spy on foreign nationals and citizens suspected of being spies or having ties to overseas terrorist groups. To install a wiretap on a suspected terrorist's phone, agents must prove to the court that the individual is an "agent of a foreign power." Some agents interviewed by Greg Krikorian of the *Los Angeles Times* maintain that this requirement "often proved impossible, either because a suspect could not be linked to a specific hostile country or because the ability to make that connection hinged on court-ordered surveillance." Although this standard is less than that required in America's criminal courts, which requires a showing of probable cause that a crime is being committed, agents complained that "they faced more restrictions pursuing international terrorists than they did on teenage street gang members."

In order to address these issues and protect Americans from future terrorist attacks, several reforms of America's intelligence community have been proposed, although many have yet to be implemented. The USA Patriot Act, which went into effect on October 26, 2001, makes it easier for intelligence agencies to obtain search and surveillance warrants. In May 2002 Attorney General John Ashcroft revised the FBI's investigative guidelines to allow field offices to open criminal investigations without first obtaining approval from headquarters. In the spring of 2002, FBI Director Robert Mueller announced plans to create an office of intelligence to gather, analyze, and share critical national security information with other agencies; he also proposed a national joint terrorism task force to help the FBI coordinate its efforts with the CIA and other agencies.

Whether or not these reforms will help intelligence agencies predict and therefore prevent future terrorist attacks remains controversial. The authors of the viewpoints in *Espionage and Intelligence Gathering: Current Controversies* examine these and other issues pertaining to the nature and scope of U.S. intelligence agencies. Authors also debate the social, legal, and ethical implications of espionage and intelligence-gathering activities.

Chapter 1

Are Espionage and Intelligence-Gathering Activities Justified?

Chapter Preface

In June 1999 a special investigative panel of the President's Foreign Intelligence Advisory Board (PFIAB) issued a report documenting the growing threat of espionage at Department of Energy (DOE) national laboratories and the inadequacy of security measures designed to protect America's weapons-related research. According to the report, the Department of Energy "has advanced scientific and technological progress, but at the cost of an abominable record of security with deeply troubling threats to American national security." The DOE was faced with a problem—how to tighten security without lowering the quality of research that depends on scientists from other nations.

In his June 22, 1999, testimony before the PFIAB, DOE Secretary Bill Richardson maintained:

> A bureaucratic "Berlin Wall" between the weapons labs and the science labs would hamper the joint research they perform and weaken the quality of basic science at the weapons labs. The nuclear weapons program depends on unclassified, cutting-edge science; requires active engagement with the other national laboratories and contact with the international community; and needs overall scientific excellence to recruit and retain the best and brightest scientific minds for the weapons program.

Nevertheless, in the same testimony, Richardson suggests several counterespionage strategies to protect DOE research and technology: tighter background checks for visiting scientists, the use of polygraphs on those who deal with classified material, and document controls. Opponents of these counterespionage measures claim that they are neither justified nor effective. Those who oppose tighter background checks and polygraphs claim that these measures defeat Richardson's goal of pursuing scientific excellence; these actions, critics argue, inhibit research by demoralizing loyal scientists and discouraging new foreign scientists from coming to the United States. Others claim that new information technology has made document control difficult if not impossible and, in many cases, unnecessary.

The polygraph, opponents argue, remains an unproven technology that has failed to detect some of the intelligence community's most destructive spies. For example, FBI Special Agent Robert P. Hanssen, who sold secrets to the Soviet Union and later Russia between 1979 and 2001, passed his polygraph examination time after time. Moreover, these analysts claim, forcing loyal DOE scientists to submit to a technology well known for its failures is demoralizing. According to Alex Salkever, in a special report for the *Christian Science Monitor*, "The Department of Energy, which oversees the labs, faces a brewing revolt." Many DOE scientists refuse to take these tests.

Other commentators argue that polygraph tests and extensive background checks discourage foreign scientists from working at the labs. "There are a lot of informed and brilliant people from outside the US who come here and contribute a great deal," says Mark Frankel of the American Association for the Advancement of Science. "If we adopt a policy that restricts people in serious ways from engaging in scientific inquiry in our labs, it would be a big mistake." Discouraging the growing number of foreign scientists from working at DOE labs, they claim, would ultimately hurt national security by preventing the development of new weapons technology.

Others argue that trying to prevent the theft of research and technology by "classifying" more documents and therefore controlling their use is unnecessary. According to the editors of the *Nation*, "All this fear mongering obscures the fact that the cold war culture of scientific secrecy is obsolete. The essential technology for nuclear weapons and biological warfare has long been widely available." Moreover, *Nation* editors argue that technology has made secrecy harder to maintain. American and British intelligence agents have lost laptops with sensitive information in taxis and on trains. "In an age of Palm Pilots," they write, "the lost-and-found box of national secrets is only going to get larger."

Whether counterespionage activities such as tighter background checks, polygraph tests, and document controls are justified in order to protect U.S. weapons-related research remains controversial. The authors in the following chapter express their opinions on whether these and other espionage and intelligence-gathering activities are justified.

CIA Espionage and Intelligence-Gathering Activities Are Justified

by Ernest W. Lefever

About the author: *Ernest W. Lefever is founder of the Ethics and Public Policy Center and author of* The CIA and the American Ethic.

Since [the terrorist attacks of] September 11, 2001, Americans have grown more aware of the Central Intelligence Agency's singular contribution to our war against terrorism. In Afghanistan, the CIA has provided vital strategic and tactical information for U.S. and allied troops in their efforts to destroy the elusive and entrenched Taliban and al-Qaida[1] fighters. These fanatical terrorists insist that the deadly assaults on the World Trade Center [in New York City] and the Pentagon [in Washington, D.C.] are just punishment for "the Great Satan."

Over the years, most Americans have quietly accepted the need for foreign-intelligence activities by our government, including spying and covert actions. Such activities, in their view, are essential to defend our national security and are compatible with democracy and the American ethic. This view is especially strong among our fighting men and women, who know firsthand the importance of tactical intelligence. Among intellectuals and the media elite, however, the CIA has all too often been a target of unjustified criticism, even derision. To be sure, covert actions abroad and intelligence-gathering at home pose ethical problems for an open society. It is also a necessary evil that, when properly conducted, is morally defensible as long as the cause is just.

And who would doubt that America's war against terror is just?

Espionage—which T.S. Eliot aptly called "a wilderness of mirrors"—is as old

---

1. Taliban fighters are members of a fundamentalist Islamic regime that took control of Afghanistan in 1996. Northern Alliance opposition forces regained control in December 2001, after successful U.S.-led military strikes. While in power, the Taliban protected members of al-Qaida, a multinational terrorist group whose principal funding and direction came from Saudi multimillionaire Osama bin Laden.

as history itself. In the Old Testament, we read that Moses sent spies into the land of Canaan to see whether "the cities they dwell in are camps or strongholds" (Numbers 13:17–19). The Cold War was unique because one adversary was fueled by a crusading ideology while the other was constrained by its democratic polity and humane ethic. Yet Moscow and Washington both employed similar means to advance their interests abroad: persuasion, economic and military aid, espionage and covert actions. Both were engaged in covert activities in the Third World.

Chile is a case in point. Salvador Allende's Marxist takeover in Santiago became a flashpoint in the Cold War. American critics of the CIA seized upon events there to denounce the agency's involvement before and after the September 1973 coup that overthrew the Marxist regime. Specifically, they charged the agency with complicity in an assassination to prevent Allende from becoming president after he had won a third of the vote.

The events surrounding the coup that made General Augusto Pinochet leader of the post-Allende junta sparked my interest. So, along with two academic colleagues, I spent 10 days in Santiago in July 1974 to examine the situation. The Nixon administration was seeking to mitigate the junta's human-rights abuses without reviving the Marxist threat. As realists, we assumed that the CIA and KGB, [the intelligence and internal security agency of the former Soviet Union], were involved in Chilean affairs and that the CIA made mistakes.

Focusing on events surrounding the coup, we interviewed all sides: American, Chilean, Red Cross and U.N. [United Nations] officials; former president Eduardo Frei; the wife of Ambassador Orlando Letelier, who had served in Washington; junta General Gustavo Leigh Guzman; Raul Cardinal Silva Henrequez and many others. The Marxists we talked with claimed the plotters killed Allende, but his personal physician told us exactly how Allende died. Minutes before the soldiers reached the president's second-story palace office, Allende shot himself in the head.

> *"[The CIA] is . . . a necessary evil that, when properly conducted, is morally defensible as long as the cause is just."*

After spending hours with U.S. Ambassador David Popper and other embassy officials, I concluded that whatever the CIA may have done to scuttle Allende's election in 1970, it was not involved in the coup that deposed him. I reported my findings at a House subcommittee hearing, to the consternation of several members who saw the agency as a "rogue elephant."

Attacks on the CIA

Seizing on Chile as a prime example of the CIA's perfidy, critics quickly organized a high-powered "anti-intelligence lobby," which, according to Ambassador Charles M. Lichenstein, openly sought to "diminish if not abolish existing U.S. capabilities in clandestine collection, counterintelligence and particularly covert operations." This effort eventually included ACLU [American Civil Liberties Union] activists, renegade CIA officer Philip Agee and former Pentagon consultant Morton Halperin, who provided Agee with classified information for his KGB-assisted book attacking the CIA.

These CIA critics sought to discredit and dismantle what they called "the nation's vast surveillance network" at home and abroad. They supported the 1974 Hughes-Ryan Amendment, which required the president to inform in advance eight different congressional committees of CIA plans for covert operations. This seriously curtailed sensitive activities abroad. [The late] Senator Patrick Moynihan, D-N.Y., said the Hughes-Ryan Amendment reflected the bizarre view that America was more threatened by the activities of the U.S. government than by those of Moscow. In 1980, it was replaced by the Intelligence Accountability Act, which required only two committees be informed.

The media also had a field day trouncing the CIA. In an intensive content analysis of ABC, CBS and NBC evening news programs between January 1974 and October 1978, I found only 5 percent of their reporting on intelligence devoted to Soviet-bloc agencies; 95 percent dealt with the CIA. More disturbing, the networks portrayed the CIA as operating in a political and moral vacuum devoid of threats and adversaries. . . . Further, the networks cast the CIA in an overwhelmingly negative light; 68.2 percent of stories were unfavorable, while only 13.9 percent were favorable.

The Just-War Doctrine

Throughout the Cold War, I insisted that the "just-war doctrine" is an appropriate guide for assessing CIA activities. Responsible covert operations are essential to our security and freedom because they provide a range of policy options short of open war. Clandestine action inside another state requires secrecy and deception, is usually illegal and sometimes lethal. Yet such activities are morally admissible if they meet the basic just-war criteria: just intention, just and proportional means and a probable just outcome. Who doubts that an Allied victory in World War II—with countless covert operations and massive deception—served a just cause and was morally superior to permitting an Axis victory?

"In wartime," [Winston] Churchill wrote, "truth is so precious that she should always be attended by a bodyguard of lies."

The just-war argument and common sense did little to convince critics like the late Senator Frank Church, D-Idaho, who, in the name of congressional oversight severely restricted covert operations. The emasculation of agency activities reached its apogee under President [Jimmy] Carter's CIA director, Stansfield Turner. In 1977, it was widely reported that Turner fired 400 experts at the CIA and relied on technical intelligence at the expense of human assets. This made it virtually impossible to respond effectively to the Iran hostage crisis the following year. These self-inflicted wounds also contributed to serious U.S. reverses in Angola, Ethiopia, Iran and Afghanistan. Congress and the

Carter White House must share the blame for these disasters.

In 1953, when the CIA had a freer hand, it supported a coup that overthrew Prime Minister Mossadegh in Iran and restored the Shah to the Peacock Throne, [a bejeweled throne on which the Shah of Iran sits]. For the small cost of hiring several hundred Iranians to demonstrate against Mossadegh's Soviet-backed regime, Washington helped restore a friendly one that helped provide 25 years of stability in the Persian Gulf.

Covert action takes many forms, from the CIA's provision of newsprint to the only opposition newspaper during Allende's regime to assisting the Contras in unseating the Soviet-backed Sandinistas in Nicaragua. The most controversial action—the assassination of a national leader—was banned by President Gerald Ford in a mid-1970s executive order that is still in force.

> *"Responsible covert operations are essential to our security and freedom because they provide a range of policy options short of open war."*

The moral and practical arguments against tyrannicide, which [playwright] George Bernard Shaw once called "the extreme form of censorship," are strong but not absolute. Iraq is a perfect example. After Saddam Hussein invaded Kuwait in 1990 and threatened the oil fields in Saudi Arabia, he became an appropriate candidate for justifiable tyrannicide. Such an extreme act was not America's responsibility, but that of the Iraqi people. Abraham Lincoln asserted the right of any people to overthrow a tyrant by violent means—including, by inference, assassination—can be justified when the tyrant has been in power a long time, when all legal and peaceable means for ousting him have been exhausted, and when the prospects for his early departure are dim. Then his long-suffering people have a right to strike.

At the same time, Lincoln warned that "it is the duty of our government to neither foment nor assist such revolutions in other governments." Under certain circumstances, Washington would be morally justified in providing technical assistance to citizens seeking to remove their own tyrant.

But one cannot rule out more direct means.

Two Different Agencies

In September 1991, two years after the Berlin Wall fell and exactly 44 years after my first visit, I was again in the city. In 1947, I saw Hitler's empty chancellery office and the spot where his and Eva Braun's bodies had been doused with gasoline and burned. Berlin, soon to be the capital of a reunited Germany, was again a major actor in world politics.

A German friend and I visited the former Gestapo, [Nazi Germany's secret police], and Stasi headquarters. The KGB ran Stasi, the East German state security service. Its senior KGB adviser was Vladimir Putin, now Russia's president.

Inside the large brick Stasi complex, now a ghoulish museum, we saw numerous portraits and busts of Marx and Lenin, but only a few of Stalin. The rows of empty files bore silent witness to the brutality and paranoia that had reigned there. As we left, I noticed four English words spray-painted on the wall: "Piss off, Nazi pigs!"

This cryptic, if inelegant, slogan symbolized the demonic kinship of the two totalitarian systems, each hellbent on making the world over in its own image. The Gestapo and the KGB were sinister soul brothers. Established by Lenin as the "sword and shield" of the Communist Party, the KGB waged battle against its perceived internal and external enemies. Given the KGB's sweeping powers of investigation, arrest, interrogation, prosecution and punishment, the Soviet judicial system was little more than an adjunct. A state within a state, the KGB rivaled the power of the Communist Party and the Red Army.

Out of deep moral and political confusion, some American liberals equated the CIA with the KGB, which is like equating Lincoln and Lenin. In his lofty ideological symmetry, British spy novelist John Le Carrè was fond of putting the CIA and the KGB in the same moral pod. Of course, both used deception and occasionally violence, but there is a profound difference in intent and consequences. At root, the CIA fought for freedom and democracy. The KGB fought to uphold Soviet tyranny and expansion. The CIA is constrained by the rule of law, while the KGB was often a law unto itself.

Now the Soviet Union and its KGB are gone, but the need for a vigilant CIA remains. Russia still has 6,000 nuclear warheads. Tyrants still brutalize their people, and the totalitarian temptation has not been exorcised. The "axis of evil"[2] is a dangerous reality.

Technology has changed, but evil still threatens. The enduring need for espionage was acknowledged in a parable of Jesus, recorded in Luke 14:31–32: "What king will march to battle against another king, without first sitting down to consider whether with ten thousand men he can face an enemy coming to meet him with twenty thousand?"

---

2. President George W. Bush identified the nations Iran, Iraq, and North Korea as the "axis of evil" because of their efforts to acquire and export weapons of mass destruction.

Brutal Interrogation Techniques May Be Necessary to Gather Valuable Intelligence

by Bruce Hoffman

About the author: *Bruce Hoffman, founding director of the Centre for the Study of Terrorism and Political Violence at the University of St. Andrews in Scotland, is director of the RAND Corporation's Washington, D.C., office, editor-in-chief of* Studies in Conflict and Terrorism, *and author of* Inside Terrorism.

"Intelligence is capital," Colonel Yves Godard liked to say. And Godard undeniably knew what he was talking about. He had fought both as a guerrilla in the French Resistance during World War II and against guerrillas in Indochina, as the commander of a covert special-operations unit. As the chief of staff of the elite 10th Para Division, Godard was one of the architects of the French counterterrorist strategy that won the Battle of Algiers, in 1957. To him, information was the sine qua non for victory. It had to be zealously collected, meticulously analyzed, rapidly disseminated, and efficaciously acted on. Without it no antiterrorist operation could succeed. As the United States prosecutes its global war against terrorism, Godard's dictum has acquired new relevance. Indeed, as is now constantly said, success in the struggle against Osama bin Laden and his minions will depend on good intelligence. But the experiences of other countries, fighting similar conflicts against similar enemies, suggest that Americans still do not appreciate the enormously difficult—and morally complex—problem that the imperative to gather "good intelligence" entails.

The challenge that security forces and militaries the world over have faced in countering terrorism is how to obtain information about an enigmatic enemy who fights unconventionally and operates in a highly amenable environment

Bruce Hoffman, "The Hard Questions: A Nasty Business—Gathering 'Good Intelligence' Against Terrorists Is an Inherently Brutish Enterprise . . ." *Atlantic*, vol. 289, January 1, 2002, p. 4. Copyright © 2002 by the Atlantic Monthly Company. Reproduced by permission of the author.

where he typically is indistinguishable from the civilian populace. The differences between police officers and soldiers in training and approach, coupled with the fact that most military forces are generally uncomfortable with, and inadequately prepared for, counterterrorist operations, strengthens this challenge. Military forces in such unfamiliar settings must learn to acquire intelligence by methods markedly different from those to which they are accustomed. The most "actionable," and therefore effective, information in this environment is discerned not from orders of battle, visual satellite transmissions of opposing force positions, or intercepted signals but from human intelligence gathered mostly from the in-

> *"Americans still do not appreciate the enormously difficult—and morally complex—problem that the imperative to gather 'good intelligence' entails."*

digenous population. The police, specifically trained to interact with the public, typically have better access than the military to what are called human intelligence sources. Indeed, good police work depends on informers, undercover agents, and the apprehension and interrogation of terrorists and suspected terrorists, who provide the additional information critical to destroying terrorist organizations. Many today who argue reflexively and sanctimoniously that the United States should not "over-react" by over-militarizing the "war" against terrorism assert that such a conflict should be largely a police, not a military, endeavor. Although true, this line of argument usually overlooks the uncomfortable fact that, historically, "good" police work against terrorists has of necessity involved nasty and brutish means. Rarely have the importance of intelligence and the unpleasant ways in which it must often be obtained been better or more clearly elucidated than in the 1966 movie *The Battle of Algiers*. In an early scene in the film the main protagonist, the French paratroop commander, Lieutenant Colonel Mathieu (who is actually a composite of Yves Godard and two other senior French army officers who fought in the Battle of Algiers), explains to his men that the "military aspect is secondary." He says, "More immediate is the police work involved. I know you don't like hearing that, but it indicates exactly the kind of job we have to do."

A Timeless Lesson

I have long told soldiers, spies, and students to watch *The Battle of Algiers* if they want to understand how to fight terrorism. Indeed, the movie was required viewing for the graduate course I taught for five years on terrorism and the liberal state, which considered the difficulties democracies face in countering terrorism. The seminar at which the movie was shown regularly provoked the most intense and passionate discussions of the semester. To anyone who has seen *The Battle of Algiers*, this is not surprising. The late Pauline Kael, doyenne of American film critics, seemed still enraptured seven years after its original release when she described *The Battle of Algiers* in a 900-word review as "an epic in the form of a 'created documentary'"; "the one great revolutionary 'sell' of modern times"; and the "most impassioned, most astute call to revolution ever." The best reviews, however, have come from terrorists—members of the IRA [Irish Republican Army]; the Tamil Tigers, in Sri Lanka; and 1960s African-American revolutionaries—who have assiduously studied it. At a time when the U.S. Army has enlisted Hollywood screenwriters to help plot scenarios of future terrorist attacks, learning about the difficulties of fighting terrorism from a movie that terrorists themselves have studied doesn't seem farfetched.

In fact, the film represents the apotheosis of cinama varita, [also known as cinema verité, a technique designed to convey realism]. That it has a verisimilitude unique among onscreen portrayals of terrorism is a tribute to its director, Gillo Pontecorvo, and its cast—many of whose members reprised the real-life roles they had played actually fighting for the liberation of their country, a decade before. Pontecorvo, too, had personal experience with the kinds of situations he filmed: during World War II he had commanded a partisan brigade in Milan. Indeed, the Italian filmmaker was so concerned about not giving audiences a false impression of authenticity that he inserted a clarification in the movie's opening frames: "This dramatic re-enactment of The Battle of Algiers contains NOT ONE FOOT of Newsreel or Documentary Film." The movie accordingly possesses an uncommon gravitas that immediately draws viewers into the story. Like

> *"'Good' police work against terrorists has of necessity involved nasty and brutish means."*

many of the best films, it is about a search—in this case for the intelligence on which French paratroops deployed in Algiers depended to defeat and destroy the terrorists of the National Liberation Front (FLN). "To know them means we can eliminate them," Mathieu explains to his men in the scene referred to above. "For this we need information. The method: interrogation." In Mathieu's universe there is no question of ends not justifying means: the Paras need intelligence, and they will obtain it however they can. "To succumb to humane considerations," he concludes, "only leads to hopeless chaos."

The Battle of Algiers

The events depicted on celluloid closely parallel those of history. In 1957 the city of Algiers was the center of a life-and-death struggle between the FLN and the French authorities. On one side were the terrorists, embodied both on screen and in real life in Ali La Pointe, a petty thief turned terrorist cell leader; on the other stood the army, specifically the elite 10th Para Division, under General Jacques Massu, another commander on whom the Mathieu composite was based. Veterans of the war to preserve France's control of Indochina, Massu and his senior officers—Godard included—prided themselves on having acquired a thorough understanding of terrorism and revolutionary warfare, and how to counter both. Victory, they were convinced, would depend on the acquisition of intelligence. Their method was to build a meticulously detailed picture of the FLN's apparatus in Algiers which would help the French home in on the terrorist campaign's masterminds—Ali La Pointe and his [Osama] bin Laden, [the terrorist deemed responsible for the September 11, 2001, terrorist attacks], Saadi Yacef (who played himself in the film). This approach, which is explicated in one of the film's most riveting scenes, resulted in what the Francophile British historian Alistair Home, in his masterpiece on the conflict, *A Savage War of Peace*, called a "complex organigramme [that] began to take shape

> *"The fundamental message that only information can effectively counter terrorism is timeless."*

on a large blackboard, a kind of skeleton pyramid in which, as each fresh piece of information came from the interrogation centres, another [terrorist] name (and not always necessarily the right name) would be entered." That this system proved tactically effective there is no doubt. The problem was that it thoroughly depended on, and therefore actively encouraged, widespread human-rights abuses, including torture.

Massu and his men—like their celluloid counterparts—were not particularly concerned about this. They justified their means of obtaining intelligence with utilitarian, cost-benefit arguments. Extraordinary measures were legitimized by extraordinary circumstances. The exculpatory philosophy embraced by the French Paras is best summed up by Massu's uncompromising belief that "the innocent [that is, the next victims of terrorist attacks] deserve more protection than the guilty." The approach, however, at least strategically, was counterproductive. Its sheer brutality alienated the native Algerian Muslim community. Hitherto mostly passive or apathetic, that community was now driven into the arms of the FLN, swelling the organization's ranks and increasing its popular support. Public opinion in France was similarly outraged, weakening support for the continuing struggle and creating profound fissures in French civil-military relations. The army's achievement in the city was therefore bought at the cost of eventual political defeat. Five years after victory in Algiers the French withdrew from Algeria and granted the country its independence. But Massu remained forever unrepentant: he insisted that the ends justified the means used to destroy the FLN's urban insurrection. The battle was won, lives were saved, and the indiscriminate bombing campaign that had terrorized the city was ended. To Massu, that was all that mattered. To his mind, respect for the rule of law and the niceties of legal procedure were irrelevant given the crisis situation enveloping Algeria in 1957. As anachronistic as France's attempt to hold on to this last vestige of its colonial past may now appear, its jettisoning of such long-standing and cherished notions as habeas corpus and due process, enshrined in the ethos of the liberal state, underscores how the intelligence requirements of counterterrorism can suddenly take precedence over democratic ideals.

Fighting the Tamil Tigers

Although it is tempting to dismiss the French army's resort to torture in Algeria as the desperate excess of a moribund colonial power, the fundamental message that only information can effectively counter terrorism is timeless. Equally disturbing and instructive, however, are the lengths to which security and military forces need often resort to get that information. I learned this some years ago, on a research trip to Sri Lanka. The setting—a swank oceanfront hotel in Colombo, a refreshingly cool breeze coming off the ocean, a magnificent sunset on the horizon—could not have been further removed from the carnage and destruction that have afflicted that island country for the past eighteen years and have claimed the lives of more than 60,000 people. Arrayed against the democratically elected Sri Lankan government and its armed forces is perhaps the most ruthlessly efficient terrorist organization-cum-insurgent force in the world today: the Liberation Tigers of Tamil Eelam, known also by the acronym LTTE or simply as the Tamil Tigers. The Tigers are unique in the annals of terrorism and arguably eclipse even bin Laden's [terrorist group] al Qaeda in professionalism, capability and determination. They are believed to be the first nonstate group in history to stage a chemical-weapons attack when they deployed poison gas in a 1990 assault on a Sri Lankan military base—some five years before the nerve-gas attack on the Tokyo subway by the apocalyptic Japanese religious cult Aum Shinrikyo. Of greater relevance, perhaps, is the fact that at least a decade before the seaborne attack on the U.S.S. *Cole*, in Aden harbor [on October 12, 2000], the LTTE's special suicide maritime unit, the Sea Tigers, had perfected the same tactics against the Sri Lankan navy. Moreover, the Tamil Tigers are believed to have developed their own embryonic air capability-designed to carry out attacks similar to those of September 11 (though with much smaller, noncommercial aircraft). The most feared Tiger unit, however, is the Black Tigers—the suicide cadre composed of the group's best-trained, most battle-hardened, and most zealous fighters. A partial list of their operations includes the assassination of the former Indian Prime Minister Rajiv Gandhi at a campaign stop in the Indian state of Tamil Nadu, in 1991; the assassination of Sri Lankan President Ranasinghe Premadasa, in 1993; the assassination of the presidential candidate Gamini Dissanayake, which also claimed the lives of fifty-four bystanders and injured about one hundred more, in 1994; the suicide truck bombing of the Central Bank of Sri Lanka, in 1996, which killed eighty-six people and wounded 1,400 others; and the attempt on the life of the current President of Sri Lanka,

> *"If you have a close-knit society which doesn't give information then you've got to find ways of getting it."*

Chandrika Kumaratunga, in December of 1999. The powerful and much venerated leader of the LTTE is Velupillai Prabhakaran, who, like bin Laden, exercises a charismatic influence over his fighters. *The Battle of Algiers* is said to be one of Prabhakaran's favorite films.

An Extraordinary Story

I sat in that swank hotel drinking tea with a much decorated, battle-hardened Sri Lankan army officer charged with fighting the LTTE and protecting the lives of Colombo's citizens. I cannot use his real name, so I will call him Thomas. However, I had been told before our meeting, by the mutual friend—a former Sri Lankan intelligence officer who had also long fought the LTTE—who introduced us (and was present at our meeting), that Thomas had another name, one better known to his friends and enemies alike: Terminator. My friend explained how Thomas had acquired his sobriquet; it actually owed less to Arnold Schwarzenegger than to the merciless way in which he discharged his duties as an intelligence officer. This became clear to me during our conversation. "By going through the process of laws," Thomas patiently explained, as a parent or a teacher might speak to a bright yet uncomprehending child, "you cannot fight terrorism." Terrorism, he believed, could be fought only by thoroughly "terrorizing" the terrorists—that is, inflicting on them the same pain that they inflict on the innocent. Thomas had little confidence that I understood

> *"Sometimes in bad circumstances good people have to do bad things."*

what he was saying. I was an academic, he said, with no actual experience of the life-and-death choices and the immense responsibility borne by those charged with protecting society from attack. Accordingly, he would give me an example of the split-second decisions he was called on to make. At the time, Colombo was on "code red" emergency status, because of intelligence that the LTTE was planning to embark on a campaign of bombing public gathering places and other civilian targets. Thomas's unit had apprehended three terrorists who, it suspected, had recently planted somewhere in the city a bomb that was then ticking away, the minutes counting down to catastrophe. The three men were brought before Thomas. He asked them where the bomb was. The terrorists—highly dedicated and steeled to resist interrogation—remained silent. Thomas asked the question again, advising them that if they did not tell him what he wanted to know, he would kill them. They were unmoved. So Thomas took his pistol from his gun belt, pointed it at the forehead of one of them, and shot him dead. The other two, he said, talked immediately; the bomb, which had been placed in a crowded railway station and set to explode during the evening rush hour, was found and defused, and countless lives were saved. On other occasions, Thomas said, similarly recalcitrant terrorists were brought before him. It was not surprising, he said, that they initially refused to talk; they were schooled to withstand harsh questioning and coercive pressure. No matter: a few drops of gasoline flicked into a plastic bag that is then placed over a terrorist's head and cinched tight around his neck with a web belt very quickly prompts a full explanation of the details of any planned attack.

I was looking pale and feeling a bit shaken as waiters in starched white jackets smartly cleared the china teapot and cups from the table, and Thomas rose to bid us good-bye and return to his work. He hadn't exulted in his explanations or revealed any joy or even a hint of pleasure in what he had to do. He had spoken throughout in a measured, somber, even reverential tone. He did not appear to be a sadist, or even manifestly homicidal. (And not a year has passed since our meeting when Thomas has failed to send me an unusually kind Christmas card.) In his view, as in Massu's, the innocent had more rights than the guilty. He, too, believed that extraordinary circumstances required extraordinary measures. Thomas didn't think I understood—or, more to the point, thought I never could understand. I am not fighting on the front lines of this battle; I don't have the responsibility for protecting society that he does. He was right: I couldn't possibly understand. But since [the terrorist attacks of] September 11, [2001], and especially every morning after I read the "Portraits of Grief" page in *The New York Times*, I am constantly reminded of Thomas—of the difficulties of fighting terrorism and of the challenge of protecting not only the innocent but an entire society and way of life. I am never bidden to condone, much less advocate, torture. But as I look at the snapshots and the lives of the victims recounted each day, and think how it will take almost a year to profile the approximately 5,000 people who perished on September 11, I recall the ruthless enemy that America faces, and I wonder about the lengths to which we may yet have to go to vanquish him.

A Historical Dilemma

The moral question of lengths and the broader issue of ends versus means are, of course, neither new nor unique to rearguard colonial conflicts of the 1950s or to the unrelenting carnage that has more recently been inflicted on a beautiful tropical island in the Indian Ocean. They are arguably no different from the stark choices that eventually confront any society threatened by an enveloping violence unlike anything it has seen before. For a brief period in the early and middle 1970s Britain, for example, had something of this experience—which may be why, among other reasons, Prime Minister Tony Blair and his country today stand as America's staunchest ally. The sectarian terrorist violence in Northern Ireland was at its height, and had for the first time spilled into England in a particularly vicious and indiscriminate way. The views of a British army intelligence officer at the time, quoted by the journalist Desmond Hamill in his book *Pig in the Middle* (1985), reflect those of Thomas and Massu.

> Naturally one worries—after all, one is inflicting pain and discomfort and indignity on other human beings . . . [but] society has got to find a way of pro-

tecting itself . . . and it can only do so if it has good information. If you have a close-knit society which doesn't give information then you've got to find ways of getting it. Now the softies of the world complain—but there is an awful lot of double talk about it. If there is to be discomfort and horror inflicted on a few, is this not preferred to the danger and horror being inflicted on perhaps a million people?

It is a question that even now, after September 11, many Americans would answer in the negative. But under extreme conditions and in desperate circumstances that, too, could dramatically change—much as everything else has so profoundly changed for us all since that morning. I . . . discussed precisely this issue over the telephone with the same Sri Lankan friend who introduced me to Thomas years ago. I have never quite shaken my disquiet over my encounter with Thomas and over the issues he raised—issues that have now acquired an unsettling relevance. My friend sought to lend some perspective from his country's long experience in fighting terrorism. "There are not good people and bad people," he told me, "only good circumstances and bad circumstances. Sometimes in bad circumstances good people have to do bad things. I have done bad things, but these were in bad circumstances. I have no doubt that this was the right thing to do." In the quest for timely, "actionable" intelligence will the United States, too, have to do bad things—by resorting to measures that we would never have contemplated in a less exigent situation?

Covert Operations Are Corrupt and Immoral

by Ramsey Clark

About the author: *Ramsey Clark, U.S. attorney general during the Lyndon B. Johnson administration, is an international lawyer, a human rights advocate, and author of* War Crimes: A Report on United States War Crimes Against Iraq.

Nothing is more destructive of democracy or peace and freedom through the rule of law than secret criminal acts by government. The fact, or appearance, of covert action by government agents or their surrogates rots the core of love and respect that is the foundation of any free democratic society. Every true citizen of any nation wants to be able to love her country and still love justice. Corrupt covert actions make this impossible. They are the principal source of the possibility that a contemporary American poet would conceive of the lines penned by William Meridith more than three decades ago:

> *Language includes some noises which, first heard,*
> *Cleave us between belief and disbelief.*
> *The word America is such a word.*

Despite common knowledge that the U.S. government is engaged continually in dangerous covert actions, some that can alter the futures of whole societies, most people cling desperately to the faith that their government is different and better than others, that it would engage in criminal, or ignoble, acts only under the greatest provocation, or direst necessity, and then only for a greater good. They do not want information that suggests otherwise and question the patriotism of anyone who raises unwanted questions.

A History of Wrongful Covert Actions

Among thousands of known examples of wrongful covert actions by the U.S. government, several will suffice to show how difficult the task and rare it is that truth is learned in time. For 200 years, the U.S. has coveted and abused Cuba. Jefferson spoke of plucking the Cuban apple from the Spanish tree. The Ostend

Manifesto of 1854, intending to provide room for the expansion of slavery, which was confined by the Great American desert and the new Free States, remained secret for 75 years, though it was signed by the U.S. Secretary of State, William Marcy of New York, for whom the State's highest mountain is named: our Minister to England, James Buchanan, who would be elected president within two years; and the U.S. ministers to Spain and France. The Manifesto first warned Spain that "the Union can never enjoy repose, nor possess reliable security, as long as Cuba is not embraced within its boundaries." The U.S. then offered Spain money for Cuba with the threat that if it refused, "then, by every law, human and divine, we shall be justified in wresting it from Spain. . . ." With the effort to force Spain to relinquish Cuba secret, a major chance for peaceful resolution of the irreconcilable conflict between the slave states and free states was lost. His role at Ostend earned southern support for Buchanan in the 1856 election and took the country down the wrong road. We will never know how many manifestos like that at Ostend have secretly threatened and coerced foreign concessions, or led to war.

In Vietnam . . . [on March 16, 1968], with all of Charlie Company, including dozens of robust young American soldiers who shot and killed helpless Vietnamese women and children and many other U.S. military personnel witnesses to, or aware of, the slaughter at My Lai, few would imagine the murderous event could be kept secret. Yet few would deny the U.S. intended to do so. The tragedy barely came to light through the courage and perseverance of several men. Ron Ridenhour broke the story after personal inquiry with letters to the Congress. The hero of My Lai, Hugh Thompson, who ended the massacre by placing himself between the U.S. troops and surviving Vietnamese and ordering his helicopter machine gunner to aim at the American soldiers and shoot if they tried to continue, was removed from Vietnam, separated from the service, and threatened with prosecution supported by Congressmen Mendel Rivers and Edward Hebert. Lt. William Calley alone was convicted, confined to base for a while, and still enjoys government support. Only by the sacrifice and heroism of an unusual handful did the story become known, and even then there has never been an acknowledgment of wrongdoing by the U.S. The medal begrudgingly given Thompson in 1998 was for non-combat service. And My Lai is viewed as an aberration, an ambiguous aberration.

"Covert action by government agents or their surrogates rots the core of love and respect that is the foundation of any free democratic society."

When Salvadoran soldiers of the elite Atlacatl Battalion, which trained in the U.S., massacred Salvadoran villagers at El Mozote, shooting even infants lying on wooden floors at point blank range, the U.S. government was able to cover up any public disclosure, even though top reporters from the *New York Times* and the *Washington Post* and a TV team from CBS knew the story.

It was a dozen years later before the massacre at El Mozote was confirmed, and years too late to affect U.S. plans for El Salvador, or the careers of those responsible for yet another U.S.-condoned, and -inspired, massacre.

The Use of Assassination

Just to list a few of the alleged assassinations conducted or planned by U.S. agents exposes the crisis in confidence covert actions have created for our country. [Salvador] Allende, [Patrice] Lumumba, [Ngo Dinh] Diem, [Benazir] Bhutto, with many questioning whether President [John F.] Kennedy and Martin Luther King, Jr., should be included, and U.S. planning for the assassination of Fidel Castro part of our public record, while air and missile attacks directed at [Mu'ammar] Qaddafi of Libya and Saddam Hussein of Iraq missed their targets. Still, a former [Clinton] presidential aide, George Stephanopoulos, the Huck Finn of recent White House staffers, calls for the assassination of Saddam Hussein in a full-page editorial in *Newsweek*, and there is no significant public or official reaction.

CIA Director Richard Helms pleaded guilty to perjury for false testimony he gave before the U.S. Senate on the CIA's role in the overthrow of President Allende. He was fined, but his two-year prison sentence was suspended. But the American public is unaware of it, and Chile has never been the same. U.S. support for the overthrow of Allende was the essential element in

> *"Our covert government's past is modest prologue to its new powers of concealment."*

that tragedy. For years, Patrice Lumumba's son would ask me whenever we met, first in Beirut, or later in Geneva, if the U.S. killed his father. I finally gave him a copy of former CIA officer John Stockwell's *In Search of Enemies*, which tells the story. Justice William O. Douglas wrote in later years that the U.S. killed Diem, painfully adding, "And Jack [John F. Kennedy] was responsible." Bhutto was removed from power in Pakistan by force on the 5th of July, after the usual party on the 4th at the U.S. Embassy in Islamabad, with U.S. approval, if not more, by General Zia al-Haq. Bhutto was falsely accused and brutalized for months during proceedings that corrupted the judiciary of Pakistan before being murdered, then hanged. That Bhutto had run for president of the student body at U.C. Berkeley and helped arrange the opportunity for Nixon to visit China did not help him when he defied the U.S.

So we should not be surprised that patriotic Americans wonder whether, or even charge that, the U.S. government assassinated President John F. Kennedy and our greatest moral leader, Martin Luther King, Jr.

We have been told time and again of the "Deadly Deceits" of our government, occasionally by career CIA officers like Ralph McGehee, by FBI agents, crime lab scientists, and city detectives like Frank Serpico. Major studies on the lawless violence of COINTELPRO, the Life and Death of National Security Study Memorandum 200, the police murders of Black Panthers Fred Hampton and

Mark Clark, are a part of the lore of our lawless government.
And still the People want to Believe.

Deceit and Deception

Our covert government's past is modest prologue to its new powers of concealment, deception, and deadly secret violent actions. Too often the government is supported by a controlled, or willingly duped, mass media, by collaborating or infiltrated international governmental organizations, and by key officials in vast transnational corporations.

The new evil empires, terrorism, Islam, barely surviving socialist and would-be socialist states, economic competitors, uncooperative leaders of defenseless nations, and most of all the masses of impoverished people, overwhelmingly people of color, are the inspiration for new campaigns by the U.S. government to search and Tomahawk (alas poor Tecumseh), to shoot first and ask questions later, to exploit, to demonize and destroy.

> *"U.S. covert actions and cover-ups are carried out against our own citizens within the U.S. with impunity."*

The CIA is rapidly expanding its manpower for covert operations against these newfound enemies. The National Security apparatus, with major new overseas involvement by the FBI, is creating an enormous new anti-terrorism industry exceeding in growth rate all other government activities.

U.S. covert actions and coverups are carried out against our own citizens within the U.S. with impunity. Paul Brodeur, in his recent memoir, describes the murderous FBI assault on the Mt. Carmel Church near Waco, Texas, in 1993, which killed 76 people, including 50 women and children. Writing of the FBI's Hostage Rescue Team, he says:

> The tear gas, which had been supplied by the military, turned out to be highly inflammable and probably caused the tragic conflagration that incinerated most of the compound's inhabitants, including some twenty innocent children.

> Attorney General Janet Reno defended the decision to attack the compound on the grounds that children there were being abused—an allegation that subsequently proved to be false—and that the hostage-rescue team was exhausted after a thirty-one-day siege. Apparently, neither she nor anyone else thought to suggest that another hostage-rescue team be brought in to relieve it. Whitewash investigations conducted by the Justice Department concluded that although errors were made, there was no way to avoid an armed confrontation with the Branch Davidians, and the whole affair was swept under the rug. Subsequently, it came to light that for days before the final assault. FBI agents had undertaken to unnerve the cultists and keep them awake at night by illuminating the compound in the flare of floodlights, by sending helicopters to hover overhead, and by playing music at full volume on loudspeakers. Ironically,

few people in the nation's liberal establishment questioned the Bureau's conduct in the Waco holocaust—no doubt out of desire to avoid embarrassing the already beleaguered young Clinton administration—so the outrage was left to fester in the paranoid fantasies of government-hating, gun-loving paramilitarists and psychopaths, until it emerged as a cause celebré two years later in the wake of the bombing of the Alfred P. Murrah Federal Building in Oklahoma City.

The U.S. is not nearly so concerned that its acts be kept secret from their intended victims as it is that the American people not know of them. The Cambodians knew they were being bombed. So did the Libyans. The long suffering Iraqis know every secret the U.S. government conceals from the American people and every lie it tells them. Except for surprise attacks, it is primarily from the American people that the U.S. government must keep the true nature and real purpose of so many of its domestic and foreign acts secret while it manufactures fear and falsehood to manipulate the American public. The reasons for and effects of government covert acts and cultivated fear, with the hatred it creates, must remain secret for the U.S. to be able to send missiles against unknown people, deprive whole nations of food and medicine, and arrest, detain, and deport legal residents from the U.S. on secret allegations, without creating domestic outrage.

As never before, it is imperative that the American people care about and know what their government is doing in their name. That we be demanding of government, skeptical, critical, even a little paranoid, because not to suspect the unthinkable has been made a dangerous naiveté by a government that does unthinkable things and believes it knows best. We must challenge controlling power in America that seeks to pacify the people by bread and circuses and relies on violence, deception, and secrecy to advance its grand plans for the concentration of wealth and power in the hands of the few.

For 20 years, Ellen Ray, Bill Schaap, Lou Wolf, and Philip Agee, [editors of *Covert Action Quarterly*], with the help of very few others, have struggled against all odds to alert our people to the perils of covert action. They started their lonely, courageous, dangerous struggle in what many want to think was the aftermath of the worst of times, but now we can clearly see the worst is yet to be. The American people owe an enormous debt of gratitude to these valiant few.

> *"We must challenge controlling power in America that seeks to pacify the people . . . and relies on violence, deception and secrecy."*

The role of *Covert Action Quarterly* is more important than ever. Those who love America should support and defend its efforts, against the most powerful and secretive forces, to find the truth that can prevent our self-destruction and may yet set us free.

Using Drug Money to Finance CIA Activities Is Wrong

by Alain Labrousse

About the author: *Alain Labrousse is director of Observatoire Geopolitique Des Drogues, an organization that examines international drug production and trafficking. He is author of* La drogue, l'argent et les armes *(Drugs, Money, and Weapons).*

It was US president Richard Nixon, shocked by the tens of thousands of GIs returning from Vietnam as heroin addicts, who coined the phrase 'the war on drugs' in 1971. Throughout the war, the CIA had turned a blind eye to the trafficking of its allies in the region and the addiction of at least 10% of its army was an inevitable consequence.

The connection between military adventures, wars and drugs is as old as humanity's use of 'mind altering substances'. Between the 11th and 13th centuries, the *hashisheen* or Assassins, members of a fanatical religious sect, waged war on the caliphs in Baghdad as well as on the crusaders from the West under the influence, or promise, of hashish. In the middle of the last century, French and British imperialist adventurers profited hugely from the Opium Wars.

A History of Drug Trafficking

But no country in the world has ever made such constant and systematic use of drugs as the USA. They were a weapon in the armoury of its anti-communist crusade throughout the Cold War. This is as true of the Cold War proper—the 15 years that followed WWII—as of the period characterised by the confrontation of the blocs after the Cuban missile crisis in October 1962.

In South East Asia, US narco-politics began with the operations of the Office of Strategic Service (OSS) in WWII. Following the Japanese occupation of Burma, the OSS, forerunner of the CIA, set up local anti-Japanese guerrilla groups across the border in neighbouring Assam. These were financed by the opium trade, without which, says the commander of 'Detachment 101', William R. Peers, 'there would have been no operation'. When the Chinese Communists defeated the Kuomintang [KMT] in 1949, the remnants of its 93rd division under General Li Mi retreated to the Shan state in northern Burma where, with the help of Taiwan and the CIA, they were to spearhead an invasion of China from the south. The nationalists developed the production of opium by the local tribes to pay for the operation. In the end, the invasion came to nothing and the KMT troops were repatriated to Taiwan by the UN; some units, swollen with local recruits, settled in Thailand. In the early-1960s, with the help of chemists from Hong Kong, the KMT began to produce morphine and high-quality, 90–99% pure, 'white' heroin. This was the beginning of the change from the production of a few dozen tonnes of opium a year for traditional local use in the 1940s to the production of 2,500 tonnes by the end of the 1990s; for the first half of this decade, Burma was the world's leading supplier.

In Vietnam, the French army financed its covert operations thanks to the opium and heroin trade via the Corsican network known as the 'French Connection'. The CIA inherited the trade and used it to finance its own secret army drawn from the Hmong (known locally as Meo) tribes. By 1965, this numbered 300,000 troops.

The drugs-money-arms nexus throughout the Caribbean and Central America long predates the Sandinista victory in Nicaragua. Before the Colombians moved in, the drugs market in Miami [Florida] was the fief of exiled Cubans, many of whom had taken part in the CIA's abortive invasion of the Bay of Pigs in 1961. In 1971, over 100 of them were rounded up in Operation Eagle; according to attorney general John Mitchell, their network was responsible for 30% of the heroin market in the USA.

When Congress used the Boland Amendment to veto all US military aid to anti-Sandinista forces—the *contras*—between October 1984 and October 1986, the CIA reverted to its old practices to fund its war on Nicaragua. Planes from the USA carrying arms and equipment for the *contras* on the southern front dropped their assignment in Costa Rica and flew on to Colombia. They returned packed with cocaine courtesy of the Medellin cartel. This was delivered to ranches in the north of the country belonging to one John Hull, a US citizen working closely with the CIA and the National Security Council in support of the Nicaraguan rebels.

> **"No country in the world has ever made such constant and systematic use of drugs as the USA."**

All of which was revealed when a government transport aircraft crashed near the ranch killing all seven occupants. Further information came out when pilots arrested on other drugs charges—Gerardo Duran, George Morales, Gary Wayne Betzner and Michael Tolliver—testified to a Senate committee (it sat from January 1986 to November 1998 and incontrovertibly established the CIA–drugs-arms-*contras* links) on their involvement in this particular traffic. Tolliver told the committee that in 1984 he had twice taken arms to the *contras* in Costa Rica and returned each time with half a tonne of cocaine. He added that in March 1986 he had carried 15 tonnes of weapons for the *contras* to Agnacate airbase in Honduras and delivered in return 25,306 pounds of marijuana to the US airbase at Homestead. He was paid US$75,000 for the round trip.

The Pakistan/Afghanistan Connection

Before the war [against terrorism] in Afghanistan [begun in response to the September 11, 2001, terrorist attacks] opium was produced for long-term traditional users of the drug—chiefly the Ismaeli opium smokers of Badakhshan—and for its uses in medicine and foodstuffs; trafficking in the drug was illegal and fiercely repressed by the government. After the Russian invasion in December 1979, there was no central government capable of controlling the traffic. Persistent bombing of the poppy fields by the Russians and their Afghan allies reduced the farmers to smaller and smaller areas of cultivation—and drove them to find ways of maximising the income from their crop by converting it into heroin. At this point, the illegal trade remained largely in the hands of smugglers, the *mujahedin*[1] contenting themselves with levying a tax as the merchandise crossed their territory. All this was about to change as the anti-communist/CIA/drug dealer

> *"The CIA inherited the [opium and heroin] trade [in Vietnam] to finance its own secret army."*

troika got into the act and the Pakistani military set up hundreds of heroin-processing laboratories in the lawless tribal agencies on the borders of Pakistan and Afghanistan.

The USA decided to channel its substantial financial and military aid to the Afghan resistance exclusively through the Pakistan army's secret service, the Inter Services Intelligence (ISI). The latter used its monopoly to favour the most fundamentalist of the *mujahedin* groups—such as the Hezbi Islami of Gulbuddin Hekmatyar and those to which men like Osama Bin Laden belonged—and to secure an important stake in the heroin business. Even under the censorship of General Zia Ul Haq, the Pakistani press was reporting how sealed lorries of the National Logistic Cell were seen delivering arms to the *mujahedin* and returning from Afghanistan with the opium that would be transformed into heroin in labs under the control of the military in the tribal agencies. This in turn was exported to Europe via Iran and the notorious Balkan Highway. Between 1979 and 1989, the expanding traffic of these networks was

---

1. Those groups of Muslims opposed to Western interference in the affairs of Islamic nations. The definition of this term and the goals of these groups are disputed.

responsible for the rise in opium production from around 400 tonnes to 1,500 tonnes a year.

And it was the ISI who reaped the lion's share of the profits in the decade of the Soviet occupation of Afghanistan. These it put to use in a variety of ways: covert operations in India via the Muslims of Kashmir and the Sikhs in the Punjab; equipment for the Pakistan army; even, say sources

> *"US policy . . . contradicted the country's claim to be the world leader in the war on drugs."*

in European intelligence services, for the purchase of components for Pakistan's nuclear bomb, then still a closely guarded secret.

Accused by the USA of financing itself from the production and trade in drugs, the Taliban could rightly reply that it had done no more than take over the networks first developed by the CIA's protégés and later run by various *mujahedin* commanders.

In Asia, as in Latin America, US policy in the years of the Cold War proper and during the confrontation of the blocs, not only contradicted the country's claim to be the world leader in the war on drugs, but prevented it making certain strategic choices vital to US interests: to pursue the fight against Islamic terrorism, ensure nuclear non-proliferation and to ensure a lasting peace between India and Pakistan.

A Widespread Practice

Since the fall of the Berlin Wall, practices that were more or less a monopoly of the secret services, have been 'democratised'. Drugs have become a nerve centre of regional wars in all the 'grey areas' of the world—Africa and Latin America as well as the former communist world. Local governments and power blocs, no longer supported by one or other of the superpowers, have turned to drugs to finance their wars, most of which have an ethnic, tribal, religious or nationalist colouring. But even here, the shadowy links between local protagonists and the agents of the USA persist. Since 1991, various Albanian networks have been trading heroin to buy light weapons. Switzerland, where weapons are on more or less open sale, has been an important centre for the traffic. The arms are taken to the majority Albanian areas of Macedonia bordering Kosovo. According to gun runners who have been arrested, particularly in Hungary, the arms were to support 'an uprising against the Serbs'. The emergence of the UCK (Kosovo Liberation Army) in 1997 was the culmination of this operation.

Meanwhile, as US instructors were 'advising' UCK troops [as they had done for the Taliban in the mosques and *madrasas* of Pakistan earlier in the decade. Ed.], the Italian police were denouncing the collaboration between the Albanian groups and the Italian mafia in arms for drugs deals. According to the Milan police, the biggest of the groups, between 50 and 60 strong, is that of Agim Gashi, a Kosovar Albanian who furnishes the heroin for *Ndrangheta* in Calabria and *Cosa Nostra* in Sicily. Another is led by Rivan Peshkepia, an Albanian with his own sources of supply in Turkey, who passes the heroin from the port of Durres in southern Albania to Bari in Montenegro by the Otranto Canal. He boasts of his friendship with Albania's previous president, Sali Berisha, and carries a diplomatic passport. At the beginning of February . . . [1999] an Albanian network smuggling heroin, cocaine and arms out of Durres on ships bound for Genoa and Trieste was broken up. The Albanians were trading heroin for cocaine with Nigerians in order to diversify their goods. According to members of the group, Croats were providing the weapons from former Yugoslav stocks.

The Albanian dealers preserve close links with their clan chiefs inside the country, whom they keep well supplied with a ready flow of cash. They also give financial support to the UCK, despite the fact that the latter, claims the Italian police, has its own drugs networks working on its behalf. According to an investigation carried out by the Italian magazine *Micromega*, Italian and Albanian godfathers are taking part in public demonstrations in support of the UCK and building contacts with prominent political figures in Italy. The US government has made no comment on their activities and no-one doubts that, as in the days of the Cold War, they will continue to be set down as profit and loss in the balance sheet of 'reasons of state'.

Polygraph Testing to Prevent Espionage at Nuclear Weapons Labs Undermines Security

by Alan P. Zelicoff

About the author: *Alan P. Zelicoff, a physician and physicist, is senior scientist at the Center for National Security and Arms Control at Sandia National Laboratories, in Albuquerque, New Mexico.*

In ancient Rome, emperors would divine truth by reading the entrails of animals or vanquished foes. The twists and turns of the digestive guts held secrets that only "experts" could see. No self-respecting general would take his legions into battle before seeking the wisdom of the shamans who predicted the battle's outcome from the appearance of the intestines of chickens and men. It was a brutal approach, and not at all effective. In the end, we all know what happened to the Roman Empire.

Today, under the mandate of the Congress and in the name of "national security," the U.S. Department of Energy (DOE) is using much the same technique with a little box wired to unwary subjects: the polygraph. The polygraph has its own colorful history, not unlike its Roman predecessor. In 1915, a Harvard professor named William Moulton Marston developed what he termed a "lie detector" based on measurements of blood pressure. A few other bells and whistles were added over time, but for all intents and purposes the polygraph has remained unchanged over the past eighty-five years. Marston went on to gain fame not as the inventor of the polygraph, but from the cartoon character he created: Wonder Woman, who snapped a magic lasso that corralled evildoers and forced them to tell the truth.

Perhaps polygraphers would do better with Wonder Woman's lasso than they have been doing with their box. The secret of the polygraph—the polygraphers'

Alan P. Zelicoff, "Polygraphs and the National Labs: Dangerous Ruse Undermines National Security," *Skeptical Inquirer*, July/August 2001. Copyright © 2001 by the Committee for the Scientific Investigation of Claims of the Paranormal. Reproduced by permission.

own shameless deception—is that their machine is no more capable of assessing truth telling than were the priests of ancient Rome standing knee-deep in chicken parts. Nonetheless, the polygrapher tries to persuade the unwitting subject that their measurements indicate when a lie is being told. The subject, nervously strapped in a chair, is often convinced by the aura surrounding this cheap parlor trick, and is then putty in the hands of the polygrapher, who launches into an intrusive, illegal, and wide-ranging inquisition. The subject is told, from time to time, that the machine is indicating "deception" (it isn't, of course), and he is continuously urged to "clarify" his answers, by providing more and more personal information. At some point (it's completely arbitrary and up to the judgment of the polygrapher), the test is stopped and the polygrapher renders a subjective assessment of "deceptive response." Even J. Edgar Hoover knew this was senseless. He banned the polygraph test from within the ranks of the FBI as a waste of time.

Every first-year medical student knows that the four parameters measured during a polygraph—blood pressure, pulse, sweat production, and breathing rate—are affected by an uncountable myriad of emotions: joy, hate, elation, sadness, anxiety, depression, and so forth. But, there is not one chapter—not one—in any medical text that associates these quantities in any way with an individual's intent to deceive. More important, dozens of studies over the past twenty years conducted in psychology departments and medical schools all over the world have shown that the polygraph cannot distinguish between truth-telling and lying. Despite testimonials from polygraphers, no evidence exists that they can find spies with their mystical box. Indeed, their track record is miserable: Aldrich Ames and the Walker brothers [John and Arthur], unquestionably among the most damaging of moles within the intelligence community, all passed their polygraphs—repeatedly—every five years.

A Dangerous Tool

The truth is this: The polygraph is a ruse, carefully constructed as a tool of intimidation, and used as an excuse to conduct an illegal inquisition under psychologically and physically unpleasant circumstances. Spies know how to beat it, and no court in the land permits submission of polygraphs, even to exonerate the accused.

Many innocent people have had their lives and careers ruined by thoughtless interrogation initiated during polygraphy. David King, a twenty-year Navy veteran suspected

> *"No evidence exists that [polygraphers] can find spies with their mystical box."*

of selling classified information, was held in prison for 500 days and subjected to multiple polygraphs, many lasting as long as nineteen hours. A military judge dismissed all evidence against him. Mark Mullah, a career FBI agent, was the subject of a massive, nighttime surprise search of his home, followed by a review of every financial record, appointment book, personal calendar, daily "to-do" list, personal diary, and piece of correspondence—all as a result of a "positive" polygraph test. He was then placed under surveillance around the clock, and was followed by aircraft as he moved about during the day. Nothing was ever proved, and his FBI badge was restored, without apologies. But his career was destroyed, and he was never again above suspicion, all because a polygrapher—with eighty hours of "training"—asserted that he had lied. Even barbers must have 1,000 hours of schooling before earning a license to cut hair.

> *"Polygraphs should be avoided at all costs because they undermine national security."*

And yet the polygraph is one of the major tools in the new DOE program to bolster security at the nation's nuclear weapons labs: Sandia, Los Alamos, and Lawrence Livermore. In the wake of the Wen Ho Lee debacle[1] in 1999, bureaucratic Washington, in search of a "quick fix," made the classic bureaucratic mistake: doing something first, and thinking later. It was the high point of the election cycle, and then Energy Secretary Bill Richardson was hoping to be nominated as the Democratic vice-presidential candidate. But Richardson, reeling from massive cost-overruns on a gigantic laser project in Livermore, calculated that he needed to show toughness rather than intelligence. Instead of doing the difficult but correct thing—reinstating guards at entry points into the Labs that had been eliminated by his predecessor Hazel O'Leary—Richardson elected to recommend a widespread, screening polygraph program throughout the DOE. Congress went along, and real security was sacrificed on the altar of politics.

Undermining National Security

The response among the scientific staff at the Labs was universal and united: polygraphs should be avoided at all costs because they undermine national security. The scientists reasoned as follows: first, polygraphs create a false sense of security. As the Aldrich Ames scandal showed so clearly, even when repeated many times, polygraphs are incapable of ferreting out spies. Second, polygraphs would drain enormous resources from sensible security measures and replace them with a feckless deterrent. And finally, polygraphs would demoralize staff, and threaten the vital work of guaranteeing the safety and reliability of nuclear weapons.

After days of official hearings before polygraphs became official policy, neither the DOE nor the Congress paid any attention to the scientists' concerns. Each of the predictions has come to pass. Wen Ho Lee passed, then failed, then again passed a polygraph, and his polygraphers (both of whom are still working

---

1. Lee, a Taiwanese-American, downloaded nuclear weapons data to his unsecure personal hard drive and was subsequently accused of espionage.

for the DOE) disagree to this day on his veracity. The DOE polygraph program has wasted millions of dollars during the past six months, and will squander $10 million more before the first phase of testing is finished. And, most disturbing of all, the majority of Sandia engineers and scientists who service nuclear weapons in the field have refused to take the test, and the DOE is suddenly without authorized staff to deal with a nuclear weapons emergency. Recruitment of new scientists to this program and to the Labs in general has become nearly impossible. The Laboratories' leaders are learning that no one feels valued if they are presumed guilty until "proven" innocent by a disreputable test.

But the damage and foolishness doesn't stop there. The DOE has run roughshod over the sensibilities of scientists through a continuous series of distortions over implementation of polygraphs. For example, DOE polygraphers claim that there are but four questions to the examination, all directly related to national security. This is a lie. In each and every polygraph exam, the subject will invariably be told something like this: "You've done pretty well, but there is a problem here with question number 3. Is there something you were thinking or worried about that you would like to get off your chest before we continue?" This isn't directed questioning; it is a fishing expedition, and has no place among loyal scientists nor in civil society.

Further, during the public hearings, polygraphers admitted that there was no scientific evidence that medical conditions (such as diabetes, high blood pressure, or heart disease) affected the outcome of the polygraph. Yet, they still insist that each subject provide a list of all prescription medications and a complete history of medical conditions. The reason they do so is to maintain the aura of the magical polygraph: "We need to know about medications," said David Renzelman, chief of the DOE polygraph program, "so we can adjust our machine and our readings." Really? I must have slept through that lecture in medical school.

But things are changing. At the recommendation of Sandia National Laboratories' chief medical officer, who has determined that polygraphs are a risk to the health and safety of employees, President C. Paul Robinson has informed the DOE that intrusive medical questions will stop, or he will instruct Sandians not to take the polygraph. This principled action may precipitate Congressional hearings—long avoided by polygraphers—which could finally reveal the truth about the polygraph's grave effects on national security.

Protecting secrets is a challenging task. Spies, particularly those operating within the national security establishment, are very difficult to find. But certainly we should not make their task easier with measures like the polygraph that are, in the end, self-defeating. The scientists at the national laboratories are willing to sacrifice some of their constitutional protections for meaningful benefits to security, but they are unwilling to do so for nonsense. It is time to relegate the polygraph—the fanciful creation of a comic book writer—to the ash heap of bad ideas and misplaced belief.

Espionage Tactics That Misinform the American Public Are Corrosive

by Ted Gup

About the author: *Ted Gup, a journalism professor at Case Western Reserve University in Cleveland, Ohio, is author of* The Book of Honor: Covert Lives and Classified Deaths at the CIA.

It was a bad week for the truth. On February 19, 2002, it was reported that the Pentagon had set up an "Office of Strategic Influence" whose mission included the dissemination of half truths and lies to foreign reporters and others in the effort to sway public opinion, particularly in the Muslim world. Only two days later, as it happens, authorities received a gruesome videotape of the *Wall Street Journal* reporter Daniel Pearl having his throat slashed. The two events had nothing to do with each other, of course. Yet, in a sense they are connected. Pearl lost his life in the journalistic pursuit of truth while his own government conspired in a subversive offensive against it.

The Office of Strategic Influence (OSI) was quickly shuttered amid a storm of controversy, but it remains an artifact worthy of examination. The office was wrongly regarded by some as a kind of *sui generis* experiment in public diplomacy rather than what it was—a natural and incremental extension of policies grounded in obsessive secrecy, the compulsion to control information, and a low esteem for the public's maturity and its right to the facts. That policy alternately regards truth as something to be feared or something too anemic to convince others of the rightness of the U.S. cause. The broader record suggests that the OSI was not just an aberrant experiment, but a calculated action by an administration emboldened by the patriotic fervor of the nation—and the complacency of the press.

Ted Gup, "The Short Distance Between Secrets and Lies," *Columbia Journalism Review*, vol. 41, May/June 2002, pp. 74–75. Copyright © 2002 by the Graduate School of Journalism, Columbia University. Reproduced by permission of the publisher and the author.

A Shroud of Secrecy

The record is replete with attempts to control, conceal, and withhold information whenever [the George W. Bush] administration, has felt threatened. Vice President Dick Cheney has steadfastly opposed efforts by Congress and the General Accounting Office to make public the details of Enron's[1] role in his energy task force. Attorney General John Ashcroft has encouraged federal agencies to look for reasons not to release materials requested under the Freedom of Information Act, reversing a far more open policy. The president himself has diverted his gubernatorial papers from the accessible archives

> *"Disregard for an informed public has often been cloaked in national security."*

of the state he governed to the more secure redoubt of his father's presidential library. He has also rescinded a provision that gave access to records twelve years after a president has left office. And never before have reporters been so restricted in their coverage of an American war.

Such disregard for an informed public has often been cloaked in national security. For example, Jennifer K. Harbury, whose husband, a rebel leader in Guatemala, was tortured to death in that country in 1992 by people with CIA links, pleaded to the Supreme Court for the right to sue senior U.S. officials, a campaign she began under the Clinton administration. She argued that they had lied to her, claiming to know nothing of her husband's fate, and that their deception may have cost her husband his life. In March [2002], U.S. Solicitor General Theodore B. Olson offered the justices this defense: "There are lots of different situations when the government has legitimate reasons to give out false information."

The mindset that created the OSI showed itself early on. Only a government that has no confidence in the public's ability to reject such twisted logic could have asked the U.S. networks to censor [terrorist] Osama bin Laden's videotaped messages [encouraging Muslim violence against Americans], as if his vitriol might persuade or unsettle the nation. (The stated argument, that the tapes might contain coded messages, was either disingenuous or naive.)

Then there is the shroud of secrecy that has descended over the detainees arrested and charged with immigration violations [after the September 11, 2001, terrorist attacks prompted a crackdown on immigration violations]. Who are they, how many, and how are they treated? Such questions have been designated security matters, moving them beyond the scrutiny of the public.

Those who do speak the truth or break rank with the administration, meanwhile, face retribution. In early October [2001] *The Washington Post* reported that Congressmen had been told at a White House intelligence briefing that

---

1. In 2002 Enron was accused of improper accounting methods that helped executives bilk employees out of their pensions.

there was a 100 percent chance that terrorists would strike the U.S. again. President [George W.] Bush was irate at the leak and signed a memo ordering all but eight of the 535 members of Congress barred from further such briefings. He reversed himself only when faced with a congressional revolt. If citizens have a right to know *anything* it is that they are in peril. Months later, the administration issued its color-coded warning system whose primary virtue, it seems, was that it was under its exclusive control.

And in an administration that equates control with consensus, dissent and disloyalty are one and the same. That was seen in the case of Michael Parker, the civilian head of the Army Corps of Engineers, who was fired for daring at a Senate hearing to publicly question the slashing of the corps' funding.

A Need for Truth

Patient opportunists who have long viewed the press as a nuisance and the public as malleable have embraced this war as the perfect occasion to draw the blinds on government. "Trust me," this administration says to a people it does not quite trust.

It is only a half-step from such smothering of secrecy to outright lies: excessive concealment expands into half-truths, are finally, free of fear from contradiction, into sheer fabrication. With the revelations about the OSI, the government inadvertently handed its enemies a powerful weapon.

Cynics may argue that the U.S. is rarely believed even when telling the truth, so what does it matter? It matters, perhaps not to the hardened fanatic, but to the hundreds of millions of fence-sitters exposed only to the toxic lies of their own repressive regimes. And it matters to us at home. In an age of global information, falsehoods are swept up like wind-borne radiation back to our own shores and to those who stand with us. Propaganda is "that branch of the art of lying which consists in very nearly deceiving your friends without quite deceiving your enemies," noted the British scholar, F.M. Cornford.

> *"Nations that stoop to disinformation, hyperbole, and lies have little regard for their own people."*

Nations that stoop to disinformation, hyperbole, and lies have little regard for their own people, and the manipulation of facts produces nothing so much as suspicion. In his denials, Secretary of Defense Donald Rumsfeld protested that he had never been briefed on the Office of Strategic Influence's role. But an underling asserts that the secretary was twice briefed on it. It is fitting that such an office should close with a half-truth (if indeed it can be believed that it is closed). One day, the administration may recognize that in this war, truth is the only reliable ally, and the most potent. In so doing, it will pay its proper respects to the memory of Daniel Pearl.

Chapter 2

Should the United States Reform Its Espionage and Intelligence-Gathering Methods?

CURRENT CONTROVERSIES

Intelligence Reforms: An Overview

by Brian Hansen

About the author: *Brian Hansen is a staff writer for the* CQ Researcher, *a news publication that explores current issues.*

George J. Tenet was having breakfast at a hotel near the White House last September 11, 2001, when an aide approached and handed him a cell phone.

The 49-year-old director of the Central Intelligence Agency (CIA) pushed his omelet aside and raised the phone to his ear. He listened for a few moments, asked for a few details, then related the horrific news to his breakfast partner: An airplane had crashed into one of the twin towers of the World Trade Center in New York.

"We're pretty sure it wasn't an accident." Tenet declared. "It looks like a terrorist act."

Tenet rushed back to the CIA's Langley, Virginia, headquarters just outside Washington, where he would oversee the agency's investigation of the attack.

Meanwhile, a few blocks away, a similar scene was playing out at the Pennsylvania Avenue headquarters of the FBI. Top officials hastily gathered in the high-tech, 50,000-square-foot command center to monitor the plane crash in lower Manhattan. As they watched, a second airliner plowed into the south tower, setting off a massive explosion.

At that point, recalls John E. Collingwood, assistant FBI director for public and congressional affairs, it became clear that the nation was under a highly coordinated attack. "When the second plane hit the second tower," he says, "there was no question what it was."

Forty minutes later, a third hijacked airliner slammed into the Pentagon, killing more than 180 people, and a fourth commandeered jetliner later crashed in rural Pennsylvania—10 minutes before it likely would have struck another Washington target—after passengers overpowered the hijackers.

The 19 terrorists on the four aircraft killed more than 3,000 people, the deadliest attack ever on U.S. soil. But neither the CIA nor the FBI saw the attacks coming—a failure some intelligence experts and policy-makers view as indefensible.

Questioning U.S. Intelligence Agencies

The failure to provide advance warning has sparked heated debate among intelligence experts. Some maintain that the CIA had no realistic way of predicting the attacks, while others argue that the agency should have been able to piece together the multifaceted, international conspiracy.

"We got caught flat-footed," said Senator Richard C. Shelby, R-Ala., vice chairman of the Senate Intelligence Committee. "We have got to be a hell of a lot more aggressive" in intelligence gathering.

On the other hand, John E. Pike, director of GlobalSecurity.org, an Alexandria, Virginia, think tank, acknowledges that while there were hints that an attack was being planned, there wasn't enough "actionable" intelligence to thwart the plot.

"What were the intelligence agencies supposed to collect?" Pike asks. "It's not like [the terrorists built] a model of the World Trade Center and practiced flying planes into it." Besides, even some of the people involved in the hijackings did not know the plan in advance, he says.

A third theory is offered by Eugene S. Poteat, president of the Association of Former Intelligence Officers. "It [was] not so much an intelligence failure as a law-enforcement disaster," Poteat says. "The FBI had more than they could handle."

Poteat says the FBI was "hamstrung" by ill-designed surveillance laws. "We've created an FBI that is not in the position to do a good job," he says, blaming politicians for passing overly restrictive laws that prevent agencies from sharing information.

In reality, the FBI is only part of the vast U.S. intelligence community— which includes the CIA and 11 other agencies. The 13 agencies are overseen by the head of the CIA, known as the Director of Central Intelligence (DCI). As an independent agency, the CIA collects and evaluates foreign intelligence for the president and other senior policymakers and oversees efforts by other agencies to gather information from spy satellites, communications intercepts and covert operations.

U.S. intelligence had long known about Saudi exile Osama bin Laden and his global terrorist network, Al Qaeda, which the government blames for the September 11 attacks and others against U.S. interests overseas. In fact, the CIA and FBI had been warned for years that bin Laden was gearing up for a major attack in the U.S.

> *"Neither the CIA nor the FBI had been able to uncover [Osama] bin Laden's plot to hijack commercial jetliners and crash them into landmark buildings."*

But neither the CIA nor the FBI had been able to uncover bin Laden's plot to hijack commercial jetliners and crash them into landmark buildings in New York and Washington. Indeed, only after the attacks did the FBI learn that the 19 Al Qaeda operatives had been in the United States for years and had even taken flying lessons at American pilot-training schools.

After September 11, FBI Director Robert S. Mueller III insisted his agency had "no warning signs" before the attacks. Tenet has not yet addressed that topic publicly, although CIA spokesman Bill Harlow acknowledged in October [2001] that there were "lots of threats and warnings and rumors" that an attack was imminent, but not a specific time, place or location.

"These organizations communicate among themselves very quietly in ways that make it very difficult, if not impossible, to learn exactly what their plans are," Harlow said.

Uncovering Terrorist Plots

While the CIA failed to uncover the specific September 11 plot, Tenet had long warned that such an attack was highly probable. Testifying before the Senate Intelligence Committee on February 2, 2000, he warned that bin Laden "wants to strike further blows against America," and that his Al Qaeda organization could "strike without warning."

And [in 2000], Tenet warned the committee that Al Qaeda was becoming "more operationally adept and more technically sophisticated" in order to circumvent heightened security measures that had been put in place at U.S. military facilities. In a chilling portent to September 11, Tenet warned that the United States should guard against "simultaneous attacks" against "softer" targets where terrorists could inflict mass civilian casualties.

> *"Congress and the White House have given the intelligence community sweeping, new powers to combat terrorism."*

"As shown by the bombing of our embassies in Africa in 1998 [bin Laden] is capable of planning multiple attacks with little or no warning," Tenet said.

Other intelligence experts saw clear indications that terrorists were going to attack the U.S. using hijacked airliners. For example, Philippine investigators say that in 1995 they warned the FBI of a terrorist plot to hijack commercial airliners and crash them into the Pentagon, CIA headquarters and other high-profile buildings. Philippine officials uncovered the plot after arresting Abdul Hakim Murad, a top lieutenant to Ramzi Zhmed Yousef, who was later convicted in the 1993 truck-bombing of the World Trade Center.

Washington journalist Joseph J. Trento, author of three books on the CIA, says the Philippine information should have spurred the FBI into action. "This should have given us a pretty good idea they were planning something with airliners," Trento said. "But nobody in the FBI even bothered to check whether other Arabs were going to flight school in the U.S.

"It's shameful," he continued. "The public should be furious."

Other intelligence experts say the Philippine information was considered unreliable because it was obtained by torturing Murad.

Gregory F. Treverton, a senior consultant at the Rand Corporation, a California think tank, says the attacks may have been "beyond our realistic ability to uncover." Still, he says, the U.S. intelligence community was looking for

> *"A comprehensive, new anti-terrorism bill—the USA Patriot Act—now allows the FBI to share secret grand jury evidence with the CIA."*

the wrong sort of plot. "As long as they were thinking about bombs on planes instead of planes as bombs, they weren't going to predict September 11."

Since the attacks, Congress and the White House have given the intelligence community sweeping, new powers to combat terrorism. But critics complain the expanded powers could be both ineffective and detrimental to civil liberties. Meanwhile, Congress is gearing up to investigate how the attacks went undetected.

As policy-makers grapple with the nation's intelligence needs, here are some of the issues they will consider:

Helping Agencies Work Together

Many intelligence experts argue that the FBI and the CIA might have been able to thwart the September 11 attacks if they worked together more closely. The critics blame the lack of cooperation on several factors, including U.S. laws—especially grand jury secrecy laws—that prevent the FBI from sharing information with the CIA.

With their broad powers to compel testimony and uncover other types of evidence, grand juries are among law enforcement's most powerful tools. But until recently, federal law largely prevented the FBI from sharing grand jury evidence with intelligence agencies.

For example, secrecy laws prevented the CIA from reviewing FBI grand jury evidence presented in the 1993 World Trade Center bombing case until after the defendants were convicted. That evidence, according to many intelligence officials, referred to additional terrorist plots against the U.S.

"Had that information been shared with U.S. intelligence agencies, you could make the case that we could have prevented subsequent attacks," says a congressional staffer familiar with intelligence matters.

Just six weeks after the September 11 attacks, Congress revamped the grand jury secrecy laws. A comprehensive, new anti-terrorism bill—the USA Patriot Act—now allows the FBI to share secret grand jury evidence with the CIA and other agencies dealing with national security, national defense and immigration without first obtaining a court order. Only evidence pertaining to international terrorism, counter-terrorism or the conduct of U.S. foreign intelligence operations may be shared.

Attorney General John D. Ashcroft says the new law "takes down some of the walls" between the FBI, the CIA and the Immigration and Naturalization Service (INS). "We are working very aggressively to coordinate our informational capabilities so [agencies] in one part of the government that have information can make that information available to, and valuable to, others," Ashcroft said shortly after the Patriot Act was signed into law on October 26 [2001].

Increasing Surveillance

In addition to its information-sharing provisions, the measure also bolsters the government's ability to carry out electronic and physical surveillance against suspected terrorists, a change largely prompted by the case of Zacarias Moussaoui. The 33-year-old French citizen of Moroccan descent [in December 2001] became the first person indicted in connection with the September 11 attacks.

Officials believe Moussaoui was training to be the 20th hijacker, pointing out that he "engaged in the same preparation for murder" as did the other 19 men who carried out the attacks. Specifically, prosecutors allege Moussaoui was preparing to board United Flight 93, the only one of the four doomed airliners with four hijackers aboard instead of five. It was the plane that crashed in rural Pennsylvania.

Moussaoui was arrested on immigration charges four weeks before the attacks, after telling a Minnesota flight school that he only wanted to learn how to make in-flight turns on a jumbo jet. Fearing Moussaoui's motives, school officials contacted the FBI's Minneapolis field office.

After interviewing Moussaoui, local agents concluded that he was a potential terrorist hijacker and asked FBI headquarters in Washington to obtain a warrant allowing them to search his laptop computer and telephone records. But officials in the bureau's general counsel's office refused to forward the request to the Justice Department because they said there was no evidence that Moussaoui was acting at the behest of an overseas terrorist group, which at the time was required to obtain such a warrant.

The USA Patriot Act allows investigators to obtain such search warrants with less evidence of a foreign connection. That change—along with the other provisions—will significantly bolster the FBI's ability to combat terrorism, says the bureau's Collingwood. "The Patriot Act will allow us to acquire relevant information faster, analyze it more quickly and disseminate it more broadly than we previously could," he says.

Reforming the FBI

The Patriot Act is not the only major change at the FBI prompted by the September 11 attacks. In December [2001] the bureau announced that it was revamping its organizational structure and shifting its mission. Under the new paradigm, the FBI will scale back its efforts in solving bank robberies, fighting organized crime and conducting drug investigations. Instead, the agency will focus on counterintelligence and counter-terrorism, working closely with the CIA and creating, in effect, a unified federal police and intelligence apparatus that has never before existed in this country.

"All the walls are down between the law-enforcement and intelligence commu-

> *"Critics say the FBI needs far more sophisticated computer technology."*

nities," said Assistant FBI Director Thomas B. Locke. "Ten years ago, there was a brick wall between us and the CIA," another high-ranking FBI official says. "Now, the CIA has a number of people assigned here, and we have a number of people assigned over there. Things are a lot different now than they used to be."

But critics doubt that the FBI's track record will improve as a result of either the structural shakeup or the USA Patriot Act. The bureau has suffered a long string of embarrassments in recent years, leading to questions about its basic competency.

The FBI's most recent troubles included the disclosure last year that a long-time FBI counterintelligence agent, Robert P. Hanssen, had spied for the former Soviet Union—and later Russia—for 15 years. To make matters worse, an FBI agent had alerted the bureau to his suspicions about Hanssen in 1990.

The bureau also acknowledged last year that it had withheld thousands of pages of documents from defense lawyers representing Oklahoma City bomber Timothy McVeigh, causing an embarrassing delay in his execution.

The blunders triggered a barrage of criticism. Senator Charles E. Grassley, R-Iowa, said the bureau was infected with a "cowboy culture" obsessed with projecting a good public image.

Kris J. Kolesnik, executive director of the National Whistleblower Center, says the FBI has not yet overcome cultural problems that have plagued it for many years and will have a tough time adjusting to its new mission.

"[The bureau] is essentially waging two wars at the same time: one against terrorism and one against [its] own bureaucracy," Kolesnik said. "They are not geared up for the prevention of anything. They are geared up to arrest someone after a crime has been committed."

Still other critics say the FBI needs far more sophisticated computer technology, first to be able to access information contained in other government data bases and then to crunch all the millions of pieces of information it obtains to detect patterns and eventual leads to suspected terrorists.

Meanwhile, across the Potomac River in suburban Virginia, organizational changes have been proposed for intelligence-gathering operations at the CIA and the Pentagon. A presidentially appointed panel has recommended that three electronic intelligence agencies currently under military control be transferred to the CIA, and that the DCI be allowed to focus on overseeing intelligence gathering without having to also manage the CIA.

Supporters of the plan say it would bring more continuity to the intelligence-collection and analysis processes.

But critics question whether the three agencies should be moved, given the CIA's recent track record. Gary J. Schmidt, executive director of the conservative think tank Project for the New American Century, says, "Given the failures of those intelligence elements headed by the DCI over the past months—and indeed decade—it seems ludicrous that we would now hand over even more power to that office. Rather than increasing the DCI's authority, we should be demanding that he first put his own house in order."

Improving Covert Operations

Robert David Steele, a former CIA agent who now runs an intelligence-consulting firm in Oakton, Virginia, says the agency is "absolutely" culpable for failing to unearth the September 11 hijacking scheme and that the agency and its sister agencies have become too "politicized" to do their work.

"I don't think President [George W.] Bush or Vice President [Dick] Cheney realize just how bad their intelligence system is," says Steele, who has written several books and articles on the intelligence community. "Sept. 11 showed how bad it has gotten."

Steele is especially critical of the CIA's covert-operations division, which he calls a "decrepit, dysfunctional organization that's totally incapable of penetrating any terrorist groups." The vast majority of the CIA's foreign operatives work out of U.S. embassies under "official" cover as diplomatic liaisons to their host governments, he points out. Many are recent college graduates with little experience in the languages, customs and culture of the countries in which they are working, he adds. Such agents simply have no chance of infiltrating terrorist organizations like Al Qaeda, Steele says.

"When you're a young person bouncing in and out of an official installation [e.g., an embassy] and you're working on weekends and spending more money than the political counsel, how hard is it for someone to figure out [that you're with the CIA]?" Steele asks.

> *"Intelligence gathering is a nitty-gritty, dirty business . . . and you have to work with the kind of people you might not have over for dinner."*

The CIA really needs older, "mid-career professionals" who are "world-class experts in specific regions, languages and topical areas," he says. Instead of being diplomatic attachés, they should develop "non-official cover" so they can get close to active terrorist cells, Steele says.

Reuel Marc Gerecht, a former CIA agent and an expert on Middle East issues, echoes Steele's point. "Westerners cannot visit the cinder-block, mud-brick side of the Muslim world—whence bin Laden's foot soldiers mostly come—without announcing who they are," Gerecht wrote recently. "No case officer stationed in Pakistan can penetrate the Afghan communities in Peshawar or the Northwest Frontier's numerous religious schools . . . and seriously expect to gather useful information about radical Islamic terrorism—let alone recruit foreign agents."

Steven Aftergood, a senior research analyst at the Federation of American Scientists, which studies national security issues, concedes that the CIA is badly in need of reform. He cautions, however, that it is extremely risky to place CIA operatives in foreign countries without providing them with official diplomatic cover.

"You're legally vulnerable [without such cover]," he says, "because you lose diplomatic immunity. It's also very difficult and expensive to establish a persuasive type of [non-official] cover."

Acquiring Human Intelligence

The September 11 terrorist attacks reignited a longstanding debate over how the CIA acquires "human" intelligence, or HUMINT. The CIA's clandestine division has long collected HUMINT by paying or otherwise inducing foreign nationals to disclose sensitive information. Some of these informants—known as "assets"—have provided valuable information on matters of national security. But others—especially those linked to drug-running and human rights abuses—have embroiled the agency and government in scandal and disrepute.

Over the years, Congress and the CIA have taken steps to prohibit the recruitment of so-called "dirty" assets. In the mid-1990s, for example, following a scandalous CIA incident in Guatemala—in which CIA informant Army Colonel Julio Roberto Alpirez reportedly participated in killing an American civilian and a Guatemalan opposition leader—then-CIA Director John M. Deutch culled several unsavory informants from the agency's payroll.

Deutch also put forth a set of rules—known as the "Deutch Guidelines"—requiring field agents to get permission from headquarters before hiring questionable sources. Although the policy initially was implemented largely in response to congressional reaction to the Alpirez affair, today many lawmakers and intelligence experts complain Deutch severely hampered the CIA's ability to gather the kind of information needed to thwart the September 11 attacks.

"The Deutch guidelines had a devastating effect on intelligence gathering," said Representative Doug Bereuter, R-Neb., vice chairman of the House Intelligence Committee. "They've had a chilling effect on the recruiting efforts of field agents. It's very clear from talking to agents that they don't want to risk their reputation or promotability by promoting the recruitment of someone with dirty hands. And it is nigh on impossible to penetrate these [terrorist] organizations unless we have people who have been involved with them."

Representative Larry Combest, R-Texas, the committee's chairman during the

Deutch era, agrees. "Intelligence gathering is a nitty-gritty, dirty business," he said, "and you have to work with the kind of people you might not have over for dinner."

The CIA maintains, however, that it has never turned down the opportunity to recruit potentially valuable informants because they had questionable backgrounds. Harlow says the agency continues dealing with assets with sleazy backgrounds, "because we know better than anyone else that's who you need to deal with in order to get the information you need on terrorism."

> *"Combating terrorism with targeted assassinations is more humane than a full-scale military assault because it produces fewer civilian casualties."*

The Deutch guidelines only served to keep CIA field agents on their toes, Harlow says. "We're just trying to protect our people," he said.

Melvin Goodman, a former CIA officer who teaches at the National War College, calls the flap over the Deutch guidelines a "red herring." The "thugs" who were scrubbed off the CIA's asset list as a result of the Deutch directive "weren't providing anything of utility, anyway," Goodman says. Still, he agrees that the CIA's clandestine service is badly in need of reform.

"Until we get a [covert operations division] that can operate outside of the embassies either without cover or with a different kind of cover—which entails great risk—I don't think we're ever going to have a great deal of success" infiltrating terrorist groups, Goodman says.

The CIA's Harlow acknowledges the difficulty of infiltrating terrorist groups and that it can be "difficult if not impossible" for agents to learn exactly where and when terrorists might strike. But he rejects the notion that the agency's covert operations division is averse to taking risks.

"You generally hear that from armchair critics [or] alumni who haven't been in the agency for years and have no way of knowing the way operations are now conducted," Harlow said. "There are very risky operations going on as we speak, and there have been for quite some time. This is a very dangerous business."

Assassinations

President Bush touched off a lively debate among government officials and intelligence experts when he declared on September 17, [2001], that bin Laden would be brought to justice "dead or alive." The declaration raised questions about the longstanding U.S. policy against assassinating foreign nationals.

The policy was instituted in 1976, after a series of bungled CIA assassination attempts against Cuban President Fidel Castro and other foreign leaders. According to an executive order signed by President Gerald R. Ford: "No employee of the United States Government shall engage in, or conspire to engage in, political assassination." Ford issued the order after a congressional committee publicly lambasted the assassination attempts.

President Ronald Reagan expanded the ban in 1981, barring all types of assassinations—not just those carried out for "political" purposes—including those carried out by any person working "on behalf of" the U.S. government.

Asked if Bush's September 17 remarks meant that the administration was rescinding the 25-year-old assassination ban, Secretary of State Colin L. Powell said, "Everything is under review."

Bush subsequently signed a classified legal memorandum, or "finding," authorizing the CIA to conduct covert operations expressly aimed at killing specific individuals linked to terrorism. Bush's action reportedly broadens the class of potential assassination targets beyond bin Laden and his top lieutenants, as well as beyond the geographical boundaries of the war in Afghanistan.

Senator Bob Graham, D-Fla., chairman of the Senate Intelligence Committee, says assassination "should be an option that's available to the president" in "appropriate case," such as terrorist attacks against U.S. interest. "We have to have the authority to assassinate people before they can assassinate us," Graham says.

Senator Shelby, the senior Republican member of Graham's committee, fears that rescinding the assassination ban might lead to a wave of retaliatory strikes against U.S. leaders and American citizens. "I don't know were we'd be standing in the world if . . . there were stepped-up attempts to assassinate a lot of our people," Shelby said.

Goodman, the War College professor, shares Shelby's concerns. That risk would be especially high if the CIA attempts to knock off foreign leaders, such as Iraqi President Saddam Hussein, Goodman says.

"The ban must be continued," Goodman says. "If the CIA gets more aggressive in places outside of Afghanistan. I think American officials who travel are going to feel the effects."

John C. Gannon, a former deputy director for intelligence at the CIA, supports lifting the assassination ban if the CIA has the full backing of Congress and the White House. "You've got to have the political levels behind you so the intelligence officers are not left hanging," Gannon said. "With explicit authority, I think that case officers are capable of [targeted killing] and would follow instructions, and would, I think, have the capability of succeeding."

But many intelligence experts question the CIA's ability to assassinate terrorist leaders or their supporters. Frederick P. Hitz, the CIA's inspector general from 1990 to 1998, doesn't think the agency is up to the task. "The CIA is an organization of bureaucrats," Hitz said. "This is not what intelligence officers do. They're not trained for it."

Some experts argue that the United States should emulate the Israeli government, which routinely assassinates leaders of the various Palestinian groups that carry out suicide bombings within its borders and the occupied territories. In the last 16 months alone, Israel has tracked and killed more than 50 Palestinians it considered to be terrorists.

Some experts maintain that combating terrorism with targeted assassinations is more humane than a full-scale military assault because it produces fewer civilian casualties. Ely Karmon, a senior researcher at the Israel-based International Policy Institute for Counter-Terrorism, said an assassination campaign "is the most efficient and moral act of war."

"You are fighting directly those who are involved in terrorism, not bombing indiscriminately," Karmon said.

Still, as the United States continues to wage war against terrorism, many intelligence experts view the assassination ban as largely irrelevant. Mark M. Lowenthal, an intelligence expert at SRA International, a high-tech security consulting company, opposes assassinating foreign leaders for political purposes but views the assassination ban as meaningless after September 11.

"I don't think it's pertinent in terms of the current struggle," Lowenthal says. "We're at war, and bin Laden is a combatant. He can be killed."

The United States Should Reform Its Intelligence-Gathering Methods

by John M. Deutch and Jeffrey H. Smith

About the authors: *John M. Deutch, former director of central intelligence, is a professor of chemistry at the Massachusetts Institute of Technology. Jeffrey H. Smith, former Central Intelligence Agency general counsel, is a partner in a Washington, D.C., law firm.*

The terrorist attacks on the World Trade Center and the Pentagon [on September 11, 2001], understandably provoked two reactions—that this was the worst intelligence failure in recent U.S. history and that U.S. intelligence gathering and analysis must be vastly improved. Many proposals have been put forward to improve U.S. intelligence capabilities. In order to sort those that make sense from those that do not, it is important first to understand the constraints the intelligence community has inherited.

The Traditional Framework

The framework for U.S. intelligence was created in a different time to deal with different problems. The National Security Act of 1947, which established the Central Intelligence Agency (CIA), envisioned the enemy to be states such as the Soviet Union and also recognized the importance of protecting citizens' rights. The result was organizations and authority based on distinctions of domestic versus foreign threats, law enforcement versus national security concerns, and peacetime versus wartime. The Federal Bureau of Investigation (FBI) was responsible for the former, and the intelligence community—comprising the CIA, the National Security Agency (NSA), the Defense Intelligence Agency (DIA), and other agencies—was responsible for the latter.

Law enforcement's focus is to collect evidence *after* a crime is committed in order to support prosecution in a court of law. The FBI is reluctant to share with

John M. Deutch and Jeffrey H. Smith, "Smarter Intelligence," *Foreign Policy*, January/February 2002, pp. 64–69. Copyright © 2002 by *Foreign Policy*, www.foreignpolicy.com. Reproduced by permission of Copyright Clearance Center, Inc.

other government agencies the information obtained from its informants for fear of compromising future court action. On the other hand, the CIA collects and analyzes information in order to forewarn the government *before* an act occurs. The CIA is reluctant to give the FBI information obtained from CIA agents for fear that its sources and methods for gaining that information will be revealed in court.

Clearly, the current structure is ill-suited to deal with catastrophic terrorism. Decisions on intelligence reform will revolve around this question of the proper balance between national security and law enforcement goals. Meanwhile, historical boundaries between organizations remain, stymieing the collection of timely intelligence and warnings of terrorist activity. This fragmented approach to intelligence gathering makes it quite possible that information collected by one U.S. government agency before an overt act of terrorism will not be shared and synthesized in time to avert it.

> *"Historical boundaries between organizations remain, stymieing the collection of timely intelligence and warnings of terrorist activity."*

A word about intelligence "failures" is in order. By the most obvious criterion—the success of Osama bin Laden's operatives on September 11—intelligence and law enforcement failed to protect the public. But only time will tell if the information necessary to predict and stop the attacks was in government hands in advance or reasonably could have been. At some point it will be appropriate to analyze this question. For now, however, such an inquiry would only distract government agents and analysts from the critical task of identifying and preventing *future* attacks.

Giving the CIA the Lead

The FBI and CIA have been working to overcome the fragmentation of counterterrorism intelligence efforts through personnel exchanges and joint training. Yet the FBI and the intelligence community still have separate counterterrorism centers. This duplication hardly makes sense. In an era when national security must be the preeminent concern, the director of central intelligence (DCI) should manage a single National Counterterrorism Center that plans intelligence collection for all agencies and produces analysis derived from all sources of intelligence. A committee chaired by the DCI and including the national security advisor, the director of the new Office of Homeland Security, and the attorney general should set the agenda for these activities.

The security services of friendly nations are important sources of information for U.S. intelligence; they know their neighborhoods and have access that U.S. agencies do not. At present, the CIA, NSA, DIA, FBI, and the Drug Enforcement Administration have separate agreements with foreign counterpart organizations to obtain information. These efforts should be coordinated. The DCI's authority and responsibility to plan, monitor, and approve arrangements between all intelligence agencies and their foreign counterparts on all intelligence matters, including counterterrorism matters, should be clarified and strictly enforced.

Judging by their . . . articles, some editorial writers apparently believe the collection of intelligence through technical means such as communications intercepts and imagery is not important in the fight against terrorist organizations. In fact, cooperation between human and technical intelligence, especially communications intelligence, makes both stronger. Human sources, or HUMINT, can provide access to valuable signals intelligence, which incorporates primarily voice and data communications intelligence. Com-

> *"Cooperation between human and technical intelligence, especially communications intelligence, makes both stronger."*

munications intercepts can validate information provided by a human source. Any operation undertaken in a hostile environment is made safer if communications surveillance is possible. Currently, the NSA, which is under the authority of the secretary of defense, carries out communications intelligence, and the CIA carries our human intelligence, which is under the authority of the DCI. The secretary of defense and the DCI share authority for setting foreign collection priorities. In the case of foreign threats within the United States, the FBI has primary responsibility for setting collection priorities. Here again, the fragmentation makes no sense when considering the global terrorist threat. The new antiterrorism law took a good first step toward remedying this problem by clarifying the DCI's lead role in setting priorities for wiretaps under the Foreign Intelligence Surveillance Act (FISA) and disseminating the resulting information.

In addition, the [George W.] Bush administration's current review of intelligence, under the leadership of former National Security Advisor Brent Scowcroft, should recommend greater centralization of intelligence collection and analysis under the DCI. Inevitably, strengthening the authority of the DCI will raise the question of whether this position should be separated from the position of head of the CIA. If the DCI is given budgetary, planning, and management authority over the agencies that are responsible for national-level intelligence, then the positions should be separated, just as the secretary of defense sits above the individual services.

Strengthening Covert Action

Fragmentation also impairs covert action—activities the United States undertakes to achieve objectives without attribution. Such action has been associated with past CIA efforts to overthrow, in peacetime, political regimes considered a threat to the United States. The future purpose of covert action will be quite different: to destroy terrorist cells and facilities that may produce or store weapons of mass destruction. The distinction between CIA-sponsored covert action and military special operations will become much less relevant, if it is relevant at all. For larger paramilitary operations, a permanent planning staff under the leadership of the secretary of defense, including CIA and FBI staff members, should be put in place to strengthen counterterrorism covert action. . . .

Law requires both a presidential finding and reporting to Congress of all CIA covert action. No such rule governs covert military operations. In the fight against terrorists, the CIA and the military will be called to conduct joint covert operations, but the differing approval and reporting requirements of these organizations can hamper cooperation. Congress should consider streamlining the law to remove the artificial distinction.

The September 11 attacks renewed questioning about the adequacy of U.S. human intelligence capability. Use of spies is an essential aspect of combating terrorism, and the intelligence community has neither ignored human intelligence nor neglected to target terrorist groups such as Osama bin Laden's al Qaeda [terrorist] organization. Indeed, there have been notable successes in penetrating terrorist groups and preventing planned terrorist acts, but because they were successes they did not come to the public's attention.

Strengthening human intelligence has been a priority of all DCIs. But human intelligence collection is not a silver bullet that can be separated from other intelligence activities and improved overnight. It takes a long time to build a team of experts who understands the language, culture, politics, society, and economic circumstances surrounding terrorist groups. Furthermore, neither bin Laden nor any other terrorist is likely to confide a full operational plan to a single individual, no matter how carefully placed as a source. Spying requires great skill and discipline, something that cannot be achieved quickly or by throwing money at it. To be sure, the morale of the operations directorate hit an unacceptable low in the early and mid-1990s. But

> *"For larger paramilitary operations, a permanent planning staff . . . should be put in place to strengthen counterterrorism covert action."*

this was not due to reduced budgets or lack of presidential support. The poor morale was due to the discovery within the CIA's ranks of Soviet spy Aldrich Ames in 1994, the revelation of CIA activity in Paris in 1995, frequent investigations by Congress and the CIA's own inspector general, and other events that indicated that professional standards had slipped badly.

HUMINT depends critically on other intelligence efforts. It is generally not decisive by itself, but must be combined with all other sources of information. A prerequisite for good human intelligence is a thorough understanding of the sources of terrorism, and much of this kind of information can be obtained from open sources such as local newspapers in the communities that spawn and protect terrorist organizations. Such analytic information is essential for planning collection strategies, successfully penetrating terrorist groups, and mounting covert operations to disrupt terrorist activities and facilities. Successful human intelligence operations rely critically on intelligence analysis to target their efforts. Thus, rather than creating a separate clandestine service, as some have proposed, the United States should support a stronger, seamless partnership between the CIA's operations and intelligence directorates.

Changing the Rules

The recent terrorist attacks gave new momentum to a debate over three controversial rules governing CIA operations. The first of these governs how CIA case officers in the field may recruit agents. In 1995, the CIA established a policy requiring the Directorate of Operations headquarters to approve the recruitment of sources believed to have serious criminal or abusive human rights records. The officials apply a simple balancing test: Is the potential gain from the information obtained worth the cost that might be associated with doing business with a person who may be a murderer, rapist, or the like? Some believe this rule has constrained case officers from recruiting agents inside terrorist groups and therefore made it harder to predict and preempt terrorist acts, although senior CIA officials maintain that the rules have not reduced the quality or quantity of counterterrorism intelligence. Congress recently considered legislation directing the DCI to revoke the rule, but it ultimately enacted a "sense of the Congress" provision, as part of the new antiterrorism law, encouraging intelligence officers to "make every effort" to "establish relationships" with such individuals.

There are two reasons such rules are necessary. First and most important, case officers have been and will continue to be vulnerable when they enter arrangements with agents who do not necessarily produce valuable or accurate information and later are found to have committed atrocities against U.S. citizens or others. These case officers may be investigated by the CIA inspector general, the Department of Justice, and congressional committees. The overriding purpose of the 1995 recruiting guidelines was to keep case officers from worrying about just this possibility of prosecution. Clearance by the Directorate of Operations protected the case officer in the field. The rules did the opposite of what was feared; they gave case officers the incentive to take risks because approval from Washington meant that headquarters had to stand behind field decisions. It is a sad irony that Congress, while passing one piece of legislation that encourages case officers to take risks in recruiting agents, in another authorized the DCI to pay for personal liability insurance for case officers. Congress seems to be saying, "Go take risks, but if later we don't like the risks you took, you will be investigated. And the government will pay your legal bills." This seems an odd way to motivate case officers in the field.

The second reason for the 1995 rule governing recruiting is efficiency. The CIA should focus on recruiting agents that have access to genuinely important information and reward case officers' efforts for the quality of information collected, not just the quantity. It can be difficult to judge the appropriate balance between recruiting numbers of agents that may be valuable and recruiting a few agents that will be vital. In some cases, one can rely on the judgment of experienced station chiefs. But both prudence and experience suggest that officials at headquarters need to review these judgments.

Another contentious rule has been President Gerald Ford's 1976 executive order barring U.S. intelligence agencies from assassinating foreign political leaders. The horror of the September 11 attacks on civilians prompted many to call for a reversal of this ban to allow assassination of a terrorist leader or a political leader who supports terrorism. This move would be unwise. The United States will win the war on terrorism, but one result of this victory should not be a world in which assassination of political leaders is an acceptable norm of international law—a precedent that could be established by U.S. action.

> *"One result of . . . victory [against terrorism] should not be a world in which assassination of political leaders is an acceptable norm of international law."*

Moreover, assassination is rarely effective in defeating motivated groups. For example, the murder of bin Laden would not necessarily remove the threat from al Qaeda. However, the executive order does not and should not prohibit targeting individual political or military leaders, including leaders of terrorist organizations, in the process of military operations, which take place during *overt* hostilities where opposing forces and their political leadership know they are at risk.

A third change in rules concerns wiretaps on foreigners in the United States and U.S. citizens (especially those in U.S. corporations set up as front organizations) who are associated with suspected terrorist groups. In addition to clarifying the DCI's role under FISA. Congress also relaxed the conditions under which courts may authorize warrants for national security wiretaps and searches. The intelligence community must have access to telecommunications and databases so it can track the movements and associations of suspected terrorists operating in the United States. Similarly, corporations such as banks and airlines will increasingly be asked or required to cooperate with authorities to trace suspected terrorists. Vigilance will be required to prevent improper spying on Americans, but it is possible to devise a system to collect large amounts of information without compromising the privacy and rights of American citizens.

Avoiding Unreasonable Expectations

A larger question underlying discussions of intelligence reform is, how much should Americans expect from the intelligence community? Over the past two decades, despite organizational handicaps and conflicting authorities, the intelligence community has built up a considerable counterterrorism capability that has resulted in many successes and, as is now apparent, some spectacular failures. Clearly, Congress and the executive branch are ready to grant the intelligence community greater authority to pursue the paramount mission of national security. And there are dedicated, talented men and women who will make every effort to reduce the threat of catastrophic terrorism. But while the American people can be better protected, they should be under no illusion that the intelligence community can remove all risk. Even if we destroy al Qaeda, other terrorist groups could also mount acts of catastrophic terrorism, including attacks on our information infrastructure and the use of biological agents such as anthrax, chemical nerve agents, and perhaps even nuclear weapons.

Fortunately, there are not hundreds of such organizations but perhaps only a few dozen, which makes the intelligence task feasible. But it is unreasonable to expect 100 percent success. Thus, while intelligence is the first line of defense, other counterterrorism efforts are also important, including prevention by deterrence or interdiction, bioweapons defense, and managing the consequences of a catastrophic terrorist attack whenever and wherever it occurs.

The FBI Must Improve Its Counterespionage Strategies

by Patrick Leahy

About the author: *Patrick Leahy, a U.S. senator from Vermont, is chairman of the Senate Judiciary Committee.*

Since [the] summer [of 2001], the Senate Judiciary Committee has been holding regular oversight hearings on the future of the FBI as it prepares for the challenges of the 21st Century. . . . [This April 9, 2002], hearing, ["FBI Reform in the 21st Century: Lessons from the Hanssen Espionage Case"], is a stark reminder that some of the challenges facing the FBI are as old as the Republic. Today, we focus on the role of the FBI as a protector of the highly classified secrets that are the crown jewels of our national security. The report by the Commission chaired by Judge William Webster, unfortunately, demonstrates the vulnerability of the FBI in fulfilling this basic function. With the American people depending more than ever on the FBI to protect it against terrorism, that vulnerability must end.

It is [the Senate Judiciary] . . . Committee's responsibility to ensure that the FBI becomes as great as it can be, and this series of FBI oversight hearings is an important part of the process, as is the legislation that Senator [Chuck] Grassley and I have introduced to implement many of the FBI reforms recommended by the Webster Commission.[1]

The treason of former FBI Supervisory Special Agent Robert Hanssen was a shocking revelation not only to all Americans, but also to the thousands of dedicated FBI agents and personnel who work around-the-clock and in far-flung

---

1. The Senate passed the Leahy-Grassley FBI Reform Act (S. 1974), but the act faced opposition in the House. Portions of the act were incorporated into 21st Century Department of Justice Appropriations Authorization Act (P.L. 107-273/H.R. 2215 and S. 304), signed by President George W. Bush on November 2, 2002.

Patrick Leahy, testimony before the Senate Judiciary Committee, April 9, 2002.

places around the globe to make this country a safer place to live and raise our families. Attorney General Ashcroft was right to ask Judge Webster and other outside experts to evaluate the FBI's security programs in light of the Hanssen espionage case. In their report, released . . . [on April 4, 2002], the Commission members brought to bear their collective decades of public service at the highest ranks of our government.

An extraordinarily qualified group was assembled to study these issues of national security, law enforcement and intelligence, and its report is as thorough as it is chilling. The findings are not academic. They have important implications for the FBI's operations in the post–September 11 era [referring to the September 11, 2001, terrorist attacks].

At least one of the "significant deficiencies" and "security risk[s]" documented in the Webster Commission's Report are the result of new

> *"[FBI] computers so poorly protect sensitive material that the FBI's own agents refuse to put important information on the FBI's official system."*

policies adopted in response to the September 11 attacks and without proper consultation with security experts.

The Commission's findings and recommendations are crucial to the FBI's efforts to fight terrorism and protect national security, as will be the recommendations of the skillful Justice Department Inspector General, who is investigating other aspects of the Hanssen matter for a report he will issue later . . . [in 2002].

Examining the Findings

This report is another wake up call to the FBI. Yet every time a wake up call comes, the FBI's institutional reflex has been to hit the snooze button. That must change. In this oversight series of hearings, begun [in 2001], . . . this committee is determined to help the FBI break that pattern. Working with the Attorney General [John Ashcroft], the Director of the FBI [Robert Mueller], and others, this committee wants to help them ensure that the FBI learns from its mistakes and becomes all that the nation needs it to be. The Webster report exposes within the FBI what the report calls a "pervasive inattention to security, which has been at best a low priority in recent years."

The report describes an FBI where computers so poorly protect sensitive material that the FBI's own agents refuse to put important information on the FBI's official system. It tells the story of an FBI where background investigations for those who supposedly protect our nation's most sensitive secrets are conducted using a "checklist approach," rather than analysis.

It paints a picture of an FBI where employees are not adequately trained on basic document security practices and where there is little or no centralized analysis of security breaches. In short, the Webster Commission found not one or two problems, but "serious deficiencies in most security programs [it] analyzed within the Bureau," and that, "when compared with best practices within the Intelligence Community, FBI security programs fall far short." The report described an FBI security system that is essentially bankrupt. There are three key findings from the report that warrant our closest scrutiny.

First, the Commission found that Robert Hanssen's activities merely brought to light broader and more systemic security problems at the FBI. For instance, Hanssen's ability to mine the FBI's computer system for national secrets for more than 20 years points to serious weaknesses in information security. Hanssen himself said that "any clerk in the Bureau" could have done what he did, and he described the FBI's efforts at computer security as "criminal negligence." Hanssen's promotion to sensitive FBI positions where he was trusted with our most sensitive national secrets—all while he was a paid Soviet spy— exposes systemic problems in the FBI's personnel security processes.

Hanssen's ability to copy highly sensitive FBI documents and, as he put it, simply "bring documents out of FBI headquarters without . . . ever having a risk of being searched, or looked at, or even concerned about," reveals serious shortcomings in both document and physical security at the FBI which must be addressed. In short, Hanssen, cunning though he may be, was able simply and easily to take advantage of the FBI's systemic security defects. Those defects must be fixed.

Second, the Commission found that the best way to protect information is not to shut down information flow completely either within the FBI or from the FBI to outsiders. Indeed, that type of reaction is inimical both to a free society and to effective law enforcement. Instead, the Webster Commission found that the FBI needs to do a better job of what is known as "defense in-depth" security—that is, identifying what is truly sensitive information, and then creating a layered approach to protect it. Most critically, that means enforcing all important "need to know" rules, which are largely ignored at the FBI, and doing better security training of FBI employees.

Finally, and most disturbing, the Commission found that the systemic problems which allowed Robert Hanssen to compromise national security for so long are not ancient history, but they permeate today's FBI. Most alarming to me, the Commission found that decisions since September 11 have resulted in "substantial sensitive source material" from FISA [Foreign Intelligence Surveillance Act] surveillance being made generally accessible on the FBI's computers to FBI personnel and then being inadequately protected.

The Commission points out this breach not only presents a security risk which must be corrected "as soon as possible," but it is a breach that also could create constitutional issues which might endanger terrorism prosecutions. This was all done without consulting Justice Department officials or security experts. The report is clear: When the post–September 11 crunch was on to investigate at all costs, security was once again discarded at the risk of jeopardizing sources and methods that are critical to gathering intelligence on terrorism and to other national security interests. Who will agree to become a confidential source for the FBI, or for other agencies that share sensitive intelligence with the FBI, if effective safeguards are not in place to prevent disclosure to another Hanssen?

I must also add that, as one who helped write the USA PATRIOT Act—which gave the FBI new surveillance powers—and as one of many who is dedicated to proper congressional oversight of the proper use of that new power until its sunset, the Webster Commission Report raises particular concern. As the report makes clear, the FBI's actions since September 11 "send a clear message that the FBI's security organization is irrelevant during an operational crisis."

> *"The FBI, facing pressing investigative needs, cannot continue to sacrifice long term interests in preventing future national security threats."*

In addition, the report raises concerns that security features in Trilogy, the FBI's billion-dollar computer upgrade, are also being sacrificed in return for short-term operational benefits.

The Commission acknowledges the basic tension between conducting effective law enforcement, which often requires information sharing, and protecting intelligence operations, which often requires restricting the flow of information to prevent compromising valuable sources. The Commissioners pointedly state that "whether the two can co-exist in one organization is a difficult question. . . ." That tension has been especially acute since September 11, but the FBI, facing pressing investigative needs, cannot continue to sacrifice long term interests in preventing future national security threats for the sake of investigating crimes that have already occurred.

The Report's Recommendations

The FBI should respond to the alarms set off by this report not by denying the problems, but by confronting them and rebuilding its security from the ground up. The Hanssen case proves that circling the wagons does not work when the enemy is already inside the circle. Director Mueller has already begun taking some important steps in the right direction, but he needs to do far more, and I will continue to support him in that effort. The Commission makes some important recommendations for improvement, and I am confident that Director Mueller will conscientiously consider them. Of the many fine recommendations, one common sense proposal stands out: to establish a system under which security lapses in any one particular agency can lead to improvements throughout the entire intelligence community.

That way, as the Commission points out, our country can establish a coherent nationwide approach to security. The Commission specifically cites a proposal for such National Security Program that I made [many] years ago, when I was

Vice Chairman of the Intelligence Committee and Judge Webster was FBI Director. The Intelligence Committee issued a report in 1986 on "Meeting the Espionage Challenge" after we had gone through the horrendous "year of the spy" with [John] Walker, [Jerry] Whitworth, [Edward Lee] Howard, [Jonathan] Pollard, [Larry] Chin, and other spies detected in highly sensitive U.S. military and intelligence organizations.

Today, a national response is equally essential given the continued pattern of espionage cases . . . [in 2001] that included not only Hanssen, but also [Ana Belen Montes], the top Cuban analyst in the Defense Intelligence Agency, who was caught spying for Cuba throughout her entire 15-year career, and the alleged attempt by [Brian P. Regan], a retired military officer working as a contractor in the National Reconnaissance Office, to sell intelligence secrets to the highest bidder. The best example of why the Commission's message must go beyond the FBI is financial disclosure. The report concludes that the FBI failed to examine Hanssen's finances, partly because of a poor security reinvestigation and partly because the FBI did not implement an Executive Order requirement for regular financial disclosure by employees in the most sensitive positions. In this failing, the FBI is not alone.

Improved Surveillance and Information Sharing Is Necessary to Protect America Against Terrorists

by Michael Scardaville

About the author: *Michael Scardaville is a policy analyst who focuses on homeland security issues for the Heritage Foundation, a conservative public policy research organization.*

The September 11, 2001, terrorist attacks made it abundantly clear that U.S. national security policy in the post–Cold War era had not paid enough attention to a vital area—the American homeland. . . .

[Since 1992] numerous nebulous issues have been deemed vital to national security. For example, in 2000, President Bill Clinton identified the AIDS epidemic in Africa as a threat to national security, and in 1995 and '99 the United States found itself fighting in the Balkans to restore "humanity" to the Yugoslav civil war. Meanwhile, the American people were left vulnerable to the threat of terrorism, contrary to the recommendations of numerous national commissions.

Osama bin Laden, [the Saudi multimillionaire who funds and directs the terrorist group, al Qaeda], taught the American people and their leadership a hard lesson on September 11. The immediate reaction by many was disbelief, followed by anger, and, finally, a rush to correct a decade's worth of neglect.

The result was a new focus in government offices, boardrooms, and community centers around the nation. But where does one begin such a monumental task? Indeed, while the United States maintained a civil defense capability during the 1950s and 1960s, today's homeland security mission is much broader. It requires a new way of thinking, one that applies national security strategizing to a diversity of domestic policy decisions that occur in both the public and private sectors.

During the swearing in of Governor Tom Ridge as assistant to the president for homeland security, President George W. Bush noted, "We face a united, determined enemy. We must have a united and determined response."

To develop that response, the president established the Office of Homeland Security (OHS), assigning Ridge, its director, responsibility for coordinating emerging policies across the government and developing a long-term national strategy for protecting Americans from terrorism. To see the importance of this often-criticized office, one need only look at how federal support for first responders [the state and local emergency personnel who are first to arrive at the scene of emergencies and disasters], a vital element of homeland security policy, developed in its absence.

The Need for a Systematic Strategy

Large-scale terrorism during the first half of the 1990s (that is, the 1993 World Trade Center bombing, the 1995 Oklahoma City bombing, and the [March 1995] sarin gas attack on the Tokyo subway) motivated both Congress and the Clinton administration to enact policies to better prepare for the threat of biological or chemical terrorism in the United States. These policies were created ad hoc instead of as part of a strategy. In 2000 the General Accounting Office criticized the lack of coordination in the federal government's efforts to prepare state and local first responders for terrorism with weapons of mass destruction. It noted, for example, that the Department of Defense and Department of Justice have targeted the same cities while others were ignored and criticized.

As a result, only 2,680 of the nation's approximately nine million first responders received hands-on training with chemical agents between 1996 and 1999, and only 134,000 received any form of federal training. . . . Bruce Baughman, director of the Office of National Preparedness, testified before Congress that "even the best prepared states and localities do not possess adequate resources to respond to the full range of terrorist threats."

The status quo cannot be the model for the future. Further, while consolidating programs or reorganizing federal agencies can reduce disorganization, neither approach will ever combine everyone under one roof. A coordinating body in the White House, similar to the National Security Council and with the backing of the president, will prove vital to implementing a long-term strategy for homeland security, regardless of the final form of the federal government.

"Today's homeland security mission . . . requires a new way of thinking, one that applies national security strategizing to a diversity of domestic policy decisions."

Today, our top priority is filling in the gaps in security that allowed al Qaeda to attack the United States on September 11. The Heritage Foundation's Homeland Security Task Force, commissioned shortly after the attacks, recommended four key areas in which action must be taken immediately: infrastructure protection, civil defense, intelligence and law enforcement, and use of the military. Over the long term, the lessons learned in fixing existing shortcomings in these areas should form the basis of an all-encompassing national strategy for securing the American homeland.

Protecting America's Infrastructure

The hijackers took advantage of weaknesses in aviation security, but attacks on other kinds of national infrastructure could have devastating consequences. For example, an attack on parts of the nation's energy grid could kill hundreds or thousands during the winter or summer months and cause mass panic. Biological or chemical contamination of a city's water supply is an ancient technique of warfare that terrorists could use with deadly consequences. An assault on a train carrying toxic chemicals could potentially kill more Americans than a small nuclear bomb.

To address these weaknesses, the federal government should first address any remaining problems in the nation's transportation systems. While the Aviation Security Act will likely help improve security in some ways (and possibly limit it in others), it does not do enough. One provision of the act requires all aircraft originating abroad to use the Advanced Passenger Information System (APIS).

A program run jointly by the Customs Service, the Immigration and Naturalization Service (INS), and the

> *"The most effective way to accelerate America's ability to recognize [bioterrorist] attacks is to develop a national health surveillance network."*

Animal Plant Health Inspection Service, APIS requires participating airlines to submit their passenger manifests to the office after each flight leaves a foreign airport. While APIS would likely not have prevented the September 11 hijackings, the concept behind it is solid.

The program should be expanded and brought into the twenty-first century in order to fulfil its potential. First, the system should be used for all flights servicing the United States, regardless of whether they originate domestically or internationally. Also, it should use advanced Internet technologies to cross-reference federal terrorist watch lists with passenger manifests as tickets are being sold. That way the airline could be notified to delay the passenger, and airport security could be alerted to take appropriate action.

Our current regime of madtime trade also presents a ripe target for terrorists. Each year, 46 percent of the merchandise that enters the American economy from overseas does so through cargo container ships. Less than 3 percent of these ships are inspected, however. As Robert Bonner, director of the Customs Service, noted during a presentation at the Center for Strategic and International Studies, "The prescreening we do is not enough, nor is it done early enough."

As a result, terrorists could easily transport weapons (or other terrorists) into the United States undetected. Unfortunately, inspecting all the cargo containers that enter this country would bring international shipping to its knees and, with it, the American economy. Instead, the United States should experiment with a point-of-origin inspection regime. Like an expanded APIS, a point-of-origin inspection program would focus on detecting threats in advance.

Defense Against Biological Warfare

Shortly after September 11, Congress and American media outlets were attacked by anthrax sent by an as yet undetermined terrorist. Americans should not be surprised by this occurrence. Biological warfare has been part of military tactics since at least 1346, and it has been used by foreign militaries and terrorists on U.S. soil before.

With the discovery of plans and laboratories for producing chemical, biological, radiological, and nuclear weapons at al Qaeda facilities in Afghanistan, the next catastrophic attack may very well employ a weapon of mass destruction (WMD). According to Senator Bill Frist (R-Tennessee), the only doctor in Congress, "The consequences of such an attack, whether it is with anthrax, smallpox, tularemia, pneumonic plague, nerve agents or blister agents, are huge."

As we learned last [in October 2001] the key to mitigating the consequences of a WMD attack, particularly one with a biological or chemical weapon, is early detection. At present, we know an attack has occurred only when numerous people start to get sick. If future terrorists decide to strike with a contagious agent, such as smallpox, every hour will be vital, as each sick person will be spreading the disease.

The most effective way to accelerate America's ability to recognize such attacks is to develop a national health surveillance network. This system should be built from the ground up and should incorporate existing technologies while remaining flexible to fit the unique needs of America's communities. A number of communities have already instituted their own systems. They should be linked to their state's health department and further connected to the federal government through an expansion of National Health Alert Network (NHAN).

After studying the compatibility of existing community networks with the NHAN, the OHS should issue a set of guidelines that communities and states can implement. As a nationwide network becomes available, public health officials will gain a broader perspective, allowing them to see unusual trends on the local, state, and national levels. A certain percentage of those initially exposed will still become sick and possibly die, but with earlier detection that number can be limited.

Improving Intelligence and Law Enforcement

Perhaps the greatest failing on September 11 was the inability of our intelligence and law enforcement agencies to prevent the attacks. All of the 19 terrorists responsible had entered the United States on legal visas, but 3 had stayed on expired visas and another 5 were on federal watch lists. Two had even been pulled over for speeding shortly before the attack and were let off with a warning and a traffic ticket.

Federal agencies do not adequately share information they have on suspected terrorists; nor do they share such information with state and local law enforcement. Clearly, no single resource can provide the police officers or intelligence agents with all the information they need quickly.

> *"One way to break the information-sharing logjam is to create a national law enforcement information 'fusion center.'"*

According to Senator Orrin Hatch, "One of the first lessons we have learned from the September 11 attacks is that we must do a better job of encouraging information sharing between and among our law enforcement institutions." One way to break the information-sharing logjam is to create a national law enforcement information "fusion center," potentially building off of the FBI's Strategic Information and Operations Center.

The center should take in information on suspected and known terrorists from all federal, state, and local law enforcement agencies and disseminate it throughout the community. Participants in the fusion center should include the FBI, INS, Customs, Secret Service, consular affairs, state and local police departments, and the OHS.

Though the participants will not receive the same information, a general sense of awareness must be the end result. The center should take advantage of electronic data-mining technology, as applicable, to facilitate this process, and more effective data sharing must begin immediately by what ever means possible. In the long run, correcting this deficiency is the most important thing the federal government can do to improve homeland security.

The Use of Military

The armed forces must be equipped to conduct traditional military operations abroad and contribute to homeland security domestically. Al Qaeda's speedy removal from its base in Afghanistan shows how important traditional military capabilities will continue to be in the war on terrorism. Further, the 2001 Quadrennial Defense Review maintains an appropriate balance between planning and capability for counterterrorist operations, traditional warfare, and other low- intensity conflicts.

The U.S. National Guard (USNG) is the primary component of the Department of Defense contributing to homeland security. As President Bush noted on February 14, 2001, "The National Guard will be more involved in homeland security, confronting acts of terror and the disorder our enemies may try to create."

Taking part in international peacekeeping operations and providing support services for the active forces encumber the USNG. It should be relieved of these duties, and additional personnel should be added to the active forces to conduct these missions. Further, the secretary of defense, in consultation with governors, the adjutant general, and the National Guard Bureau, should ensure that all National Guard units are integrated into the state and community incident-response plans in a support role.

The steps outlined above represent just a few of the immediate policy changes the United States should enact to improve domestic security. While none of these recommendations will guarantee that another attack does not occur, fixing these gaps in security will decrease its likelihood and increase the nation's ability to respond.

Further, these recommendations are merely the beginning of an effective homeland security policy. They should evolve into a national strategy, which should be adjusted annually as lessons are learned and priorities change. Other issues, such as how the federal government organizes for homeland security, should only be addressed after the most important immediate concerns are met and the nation has an effective national strategy.

U.S. Intelligence Agencies Must Curb Their Reliance on Surveillance Technology

by Kevin Hogan

About the author: *Kevin Hogan is the web content team leader for* Technology Review, *a magazine covering emerging technologies.*

As the United States tries to grapple with the new realities of war and terrorism, questions for its intelligence community keep coming: How could something like [the terrorist attacks of] September 11, 2001, occur without plans being detected? Who was tracking the activities of suspected terrorists inside the country? How were they even here in the first place? What happened to those high-tech, Big Brother–type surveillance tools like the notorious global-communications eavesdropping network Echelon, or Carnivore, the FBI's Internet snoopware, that were supposed to sniff out criminal activity?

For several decades, electronic systems have been quietly put in place to intercept satellite communications, tap phone calls, monitor e-mail and Web traffic and then turn this massive flow of information into intelligence reports for U.S. leaders and investigative aids for law enforcement. Yet despite the $30 billion invested in them, and all the secrecy afforded them, government information technologies still could not connect the proverbial dots of the World Trade Center plot. "Obviously, there were intelligence failures on a number of levels," says Barry Posen, a defense policy analyst with MIT's Center for International Studies.

All-Seeing, Not All-Knowing

Now that it is apparent that these supposedly all-seeing government systems are not all-knowing, how can we ascertain that they work at all? While the technologies to intercept and capture any and every communication conjure images of an Orwellian omniscience,[1] many experts say the ability to derive useful knowledge from all that data is still far from plausible. Even as the processing times get faster and the software gets smarter, the process of turning raw data into assured intelligence is far from perfect. If the goal is capturing, listening to and then actually [using] every single electronic communication in the United States, "In practical terms, we're not even close," says Gary McGraw, CTO [Chief Technology Officer] at Cigital, a Dulles, Virginia-based network security software vendor.

It doesn't seem to be for lack of trying, however. Today, the U.S. intelligence community comprises more than a dozen major agencies, including the CIA, FBI and the National Security Agency [NSA]. Within these bodies, there are dozens more departments, such as the CIA's directorate of science and technology, that specifically develop information technologies to aid in the practice of knowing what other people don't want them to know.

> *"Even as the processing times get faster and the software gets smarter, the process of turning raw data into assured intelligence is far from perfect."*

While the agencies theoretically cooperate, especially since September 11, there is no centralized information system to compare and contrast data collected among them. Critics claim that this bureaucratic and technical fragmentation is one reason terrorists were able to hatch their plan under the government's radar.

It is far from the only one. Even if intelligence agencies seamlessly integrate their knowledge, the tools available to them now and for the foreseeable future do not appear up to the task of providing the early warning needed to thwart terrorist plots. "My first reaction is not necessarily a question of why didn't these tools work, but how hard it would have been to discover this in the first place," says Sayan Chakraborty, vice president of engineering at Sigaba, a San Mateo, California-based company specializing in e-mail encryption.

Hearing Without Listening

Despite its . . . catastrophic lapses, the United States has a long and distinguished history of successfully using advanced information-gathering and analysis tools against its enemies. The Signals Intelligence Section, the forerunner of today's National Security Agency, came into being in World War II, when the United States broke the Japanese military code known as Purple and discovered plans to invade Midway Island. The NSA's early forays in cryptography contributed to the development of the first supercomputers and other information technologies. In his book *The Wizards of Langley: Inside the CIA's Directorate*

---

1. The authors refer to Big Brother, an omnipresent figure in George Orwell's novel *1984*, which depicts a futuristic totalitarian state.

of Science and Technology, National Security Archive senior fellow Jeffrey T. Richelson published more than 40 declassified documents that trace the CIA's exploitation of science and technology for the purposes of intelligence gathering. "From the early 1950s to the present, technology has played an essential part in analysis," he says.

The granddaddy of today's governmental electronic surveillance is Echelon, the National Security Agency's infamous, yet officially unacknowledged, global surveillance network. Said to be the most comprehensive and sophisticated signals intelligence setup in existence, Echelon reportedly has the capability to monitor every communication transmitted by satellite outside of U.S. borders—by some counts, three billion telephone calls, e-mail messages, faxes and broadcasts daily. Technically, Echelon technology could monitor domestic communications too, though that is prohibited under U.S. law.

According to a European Parliament report released in September [2001], Echelon collects information through a complex web of radio antennae at listening stations across the planet. Other sources claim that one listening station in particular, at Menwith Hill in England, operated by U.S. and British intelligence services, is placed in the most convenient spot to tap transatlantic communications cables as well. Investigations cited by the American Civil Liberties Union [ACLU] and others report that Echelon rakes these immense volumes of data through "dictionary" software that operates on a vast computer network hosted by intelligence agencies from five countries—the United States, Britain, Australia, Canada and New Zealand. The dictionary program flags messages containing any of a set of predetermined keywords, such as "bomb" or "President Bush." The words are rumored to be changed on a regular basis.

"Intelligence experts agree that the mass of information generated every day around the world far outstrips the capacity of present-day technologies to process it."

How the actual process of data sifting works remains a mystery. National security restrictions prohibit anyone from speaking publicly about the program. Quips one source who has followed the technology, "Anyone who knows about it won't talk about it, and anyone who talks about it doesn't really know about it." Some experts suspect, however, that Echelon's data processing is based on a variety of technologies in use in the commercial world today, including speech recognition and word pattern finding. "Word pattern recognition is nothing new," says Winn Schwartau, a security consultant in Seminole, Florida, and the author of *Information Warfare* and *Cybershock*. "We've been using that sort of stuff for years. But if you look at how advanced the searching abilities for the average person have become, I can only imagine the type of stuff that government security agencies have in operation."

According to Schwartau and others, the ability to sort through billions of messages and divine anything useful encompasses a number of techniques. Speech recognition systems and optical character readers convert spoken words (from phone conversations) and printed text (as from intercepted faxes) into catalogued and searchable digital data. Language translation software turns many of the world's spoken tongues into the English that the U.S. intelligence community prefers. Data-mining software searches volumes of data and establishes relationships among them by finding similarities and patterns.

"Even the most advanced spying technology can be stymied by embarrassingly primitive countermeasures."

Echelon has supposedly been using techniques like these to churn data into knowledge about foreign governments, corporations and even specific individuals, since the 1970s. Subjects of surveillance are reported to have even included the likes of Princess Diana, whose work eliminating land mines ran counter to U.S. policy. And in the months leading up to September 11, 2001, according to reports from the German newspaper *Frankfurter Allgemeine Zeitung*, snippets produced by Echelon intimated that "a big operation" was in place by terrorists seeking to destroy "American targets." Other information collected may in hindsight be pieced together to divine a much clearer picture of the operation. Unfortunately, things did not come together in time to warn of the attacks.

Watch What You Type

Another government snooping technology that has been the subject of controversy since long before September 11 is Carnivore. Comprising a set of programs in development by the FBI since 1996, Carnivore is devised to intercept data traffic sent over the Internet to assist federal authorities in criminal investigation. According to the FBI, Carnivore is installed only with the cooperation of an Internet service provider and after obtaining appropriate judicial approval to track e-mail, instant messages and Web search trails. And the system inspects only those communications that are legally authorized for interception.

That, at least, is the theory. Civil liberties organizations such as the ACLU, the Electronic Frontier Foundation and the Electronic Privacy Information Center worry Carnivore could be used to monitor much more than that.

To counter that suspicion, the U.S. Department of Justice hired Chicago-based IIT Research Institute to perform the only testing of Carnivore permitted outside government agencies. According to IIT's report, published . . . [in] December [2000], Carnivore works much like the commercial network diagnostic programs—called "sniffers"—that are used to monitor corporate networks, and runs on nothing more than an average personal computer.

After securing the proper warrants, the FBI will approach an Internet service provider to attach a Carnivore-loaded PC to its internal cabling. When plugged into a hub, the collection computer sees all data packets going by. It then copies only those packets that match settings prescribed by the FBI and approved by court order. Agents can view the captured packets in two different modes. In so-called pen mode, the system displays only information that identifies the sender and the intended recipient—numerical Internet addresses and e-mail names—and subject lines. In "full mode," the agent can access not just this address information but also the entire contents of the message.

Once Carnivore has been installed at the Internet service provider, it is controlled remotely, according to the IIT report. The collection computer is connected to an analog voice line installed specifically for the particular tap. The intercepted data are stored on a two-gigabyte disk, which is then taken back to FBI laboratories for analysis. The data packets—broken bits of e-mail messages, Web pages and any other form of data sent across the Internet—can then be rebuilt and reviewed.

While Echelon and Carnivore are the most infamous intelligence collection tools, they are not the only ones, however. Government skunk works are constantly cooking up new tools to assist in covert surveillance operations. These include other quasi-legendary projects like Tempest, the code word for a number of surveillance technologies that can capture data displayed on computer screens by picking up electromagnetic emissions from the internal electron beams that create the images.

Every once in a while, the intelligence community opens its cloak to show off some of its tricks. . . . [In] March [2000], for example, Larry Fairchild, director of the CIA's officer of advanced information technology, brought a group of reporters into the basement of the agency's headquarters in Langley, Virginia. There, he demonstrated two programs deemed safe for public consumption: Fluent and Oasis.

Fluent performs computer searches of documents written in different languages. An analyst types in a query in English, just as if he or she were using a garden-variety search engine like Google. The software fishes out relevant documents in a number of foreign languages—including Russian, Chinese, Portuguese, Serbo-Croatian, Korean and Ukrainian—and then translates them into English.

> *"Sophisticated intelligence paraphernalia still can't guarantee success when pitted against the malevolent combination of human ingenuity and capacity for evil."*

Oasis converts audio signals from television and radio broadcasts, such as those from Qatar-based al-Jazeera, into text. It distinguishes accents, whether the speaker is male or female, and whether one voice is different from another of the same gender. The software then generates a transcript of those transmissions, identifying which voice uttered which statements. While Oasis can today comprehend only English-language programs, the CIA is developing versions that work in Chinese and Arabic, among other languages. Oasis can reportedly process and analyze a half-hour broadcast in as little as 10 minutes, as opposed to the 90 minutes that the task typically takes for an analyst working without the software.

Information, Not Intelligence

Assuming all this impressive high-tech wizardry is fully operational, how could a band of terrorists, including many already suspected as such, operate within U.S. borders for years and still escape detection—undoubtedly making phone calls and exchanging e-mail with coconspirators all the while? The answers, unfortunately, don't provide a basis for optimism about the ability of these systems to offer much protection in the new war against terrorism.

First, security and intelligence experts agree that the mass of information generated every day around the world far outstrips the capacity of present-day technologies to process it. "You're talking about incredible mountains of information, and trying to find that needle," says McGraw.

Intelligence agency leaders themselves have admitted their vulnerabilities. "We're behind the curve in keeping up with the global telecommunications revolution," National Security Agency director Michael Hayden told CBS's *60 Minutes* in a rare public admission . . . [in] February [2000]. In testimony to Congress days after the attacks on the World Trade Center and Pentagon, Attorney General John Ashcroft warned that terrorists still have the "competitive advantage" when it comes to domestic espionage, and that "we are sending our troops into the modern field of battle with antique weapons."

Then there is the matter of encryption technologies that can turn even intercepted communications into gobbledygook. "The odds are nigh on impossible that the NSA or anybody else is going to·be able to break" an encrypted message, says security expert and author Schwartau. Another technology that [terrorist] Osama bin Laden's minions reportedly used [to plan the September 11 attacks] falls under the rubric of steganography: cloaking one type of data file within another. It is possible, for example, to hide a text file with attack plans within a bit-mapped photo of Britney Spears. Just try to filter down the number of those images flying around the Internet.

And even the most advanced spying technology can be stymied by embarrassingly primitive countermeasures. Conspirators can go the old-fashioned route of disguising their activities by using simple ciphers that substitute letters for numbers or other letters; Thomas Jefferson used such codes in his international communiqués as George Washington's secretary of state. Digital's McGraw says this would be the easiest way to avoid detection: "To use a crude example: maybe the terrorists substituted the word 'banana' for 'bomb,' and 'orange' for 'World Trade Center.' Do you flag every unusual pattern with random associations?"

Beyond the pure technology issues lies the question of how these tools can be used in a way that is compatible with an open and democratic society. Even in the rally-round-the-flag mood following the attacks, many U.S. citizens expressed concern about the government's expanding authority to snoop on their movements and communications. Organizations like the Electronic Frontier Foundation are highly vigilant about governmental attempts to expand the use of surveillance technologies such as Carnivore. "We really have no sense beyond a few basics they decided to reveal about how they use these tools," says Lee Tien, senior staff attorney for the organization. "They just want us to accept that they need them, without explaining why or how."

And while technologies like Carnivore have proved useful in investigations of specific individuals, they could be abused when directed at wider groups. People can quickly become "suspects" on no more evidence than an e-mail received or a Web site visited.

In the end, computer-based surveillance technologies may be best employed after the fact, says John Pike, director of GlobalSecurity.org, a Web-based military and intelligence policy group headquartered in Alexandria, Virginia. He notes that Carnivore, in particular, "was very effective in tracking down" and arresting former FBI agent and Soviet spy Robert Hanssen. "It also helped dramatically after the bombing to track down these terrorists' activities. It helped them detain at least 400 to 500 other people as suspects." According to Pike, U.S. citizens are going to have to become comfortable with such mass arrests if this type of technology is going to be used.

Even if the obstacles of bureaucracy, societal resistance and technical limitations were all to be surmounted, there's no assurance that high-tech spyware would ever provide the kind of security that people now crave. Will these technologies help recognize the danger next time? Even the most sophisticated intelligence paraphernalia still can't guarantee success when pitted against the malevolent combination of human ingenuity and capacity for evil.

The U.S. Intelligence Community Must Develop More Human Intelligence to Combat Terrorism

by Jamie Lowther-Pinkerton

About the author: *Jamie Lowther-Pinkerton, who spent twenty years in the British Special Air Service and Irish Guards, teaches courses on travel safety for students and businesspeople traveling abroad.*

Colin Powell once responded to a question about whether the United States would be deploying ground troops to the Balkans by saying, 'We do deserts, not mountains.' While it may be a little unfair to quote the General now, out of context and a world away from those sybaritic days before [the terrorist attacks of] 11 September [2001], the statement nevertheless encapsulates the problem facing his President's [George W. Bush] coalition against terrorism.

Initially, from my experience as a Special Forces officer, I thought the US had got it right. The absence of high-tech ordnance hurtling down on the heads of an impoverished Third World country in the first three weeks after 11 September gave me the hope that the Americans were capable of thinking laterally and playing a canny enough game to get [Osama] bin Laden without inflaming Islam.

Using the Wrong Weapons

Then came the announcement on the morning news that, overnight, Afghanistan had been struck by cruise missiles. Then the aerial bombing from thousands of feet up—with all its implications for collateral damage—closely followed by the first widely trumpeted results of that bombing: the deaths of four Red Cross staff in Kabul. Shortly afterwards came the ludicrously predictable statement from the Pentagon: the US had achieved 'air supremacy'. Air su-

Jamie Lowther-Pinkerton, "Brains, Not Bombs," *Spectator*, vol. 287, October 2001, pp. 16, 18. Copyright © 2001 by the Spectator. Reproduced by permission.

premacy over what? A couple of mullahs on flying carpets?

The new phase of the offensive—pinprick, in-and-out raids on Taleban [Afghanistan's ruling regime accused of harboring terrorists] military installations already trashed from the air—is as unlikely to bring peace to Afghanistan as the bombing campaign that preceded it. US Rangers mounted a daring parachute assault on an Afghan airfield outside Kandahar [on October 20, 2001]. While the whole thing was exciting to read about, I am

> *"Usable intelligence is not collected from 130 miles up, but from a maximum of six feet, through the eyes and ears of men and women."*

still unsure as to the point of launching a raid against an airfield that has already been rendered unusable by air strikes. If it was to demonstrate in a suitably glitzy way the beginning of 'Phase 2: The Ground War', then it might have served some limited purpose: if only to deflect growing media concern away from where this pointless bombing is taking us.

At every stage, the US shows every sign of fighting this war in the wrong way and with the wrong weapons. For the fact is that nothing can be done in places like Afghanistan unless you do 'do mountains'—both in the back-breaking, physical sense, and in the implied context of having to cope in an environment fraught with danger for the gatherers of hard intelligence. And it is hard intelligence on the whereabouts of Osama bin Laden [the terrorist accused of orchestrating the September 11 attacks] that the allies are clearly still lacking; otherwise why herald the ground offensive by filming something as relatively innocuous as a parachute drop on a defunct airfield?

The problems facing the CIA and others, conditioned to the sort of wizardry that can pick up the markings on the turret of an Iraqi tank from a satellite in space, began to emerge in 1999. Then it transpired that what had worked so well on the billiard-table flatness of the Gulf was woefully lacking in gently rolling Kosovo, [Yugoslavia]. Employing age-old principles of camouflage, the Serbian 3rd Army escaped, virtually unscathed, the worst that NATO air-power could throw at it. How much less effective, then, will these distant analysts be at panning for the flecks of gold when planning to strike at the wolf in his lair, somewhere in the mountains of Kandahar Province?

Gathering Usable Intelligence

In such places, high-grade, usable intelligence is not collected from 130 miles up, but from a maximum of six feet, through the eyes and ears of men and women. At its most romantic, it is about scrabbling through bouldered ravine and over sun-split ridge, talking to tribal elders in their own language, eating their food and living their life until, little by little, the confidences begin to build and the information starts to trickle. But it is also about doing nasty things: appealing to ideology, altruism, greed, hate, fear, until a source can be compromised, used and ultimately 'discarded'. It is unpleasant and morally fraught for democracies. Currently, FBI touts cannot legally have criminal records: how, then, do you penetrate the Mafia? Post 11 September we face the same quandary in macro. Do we stay superficial, or is it in our interests to go for substance and become democracies with teeth?

President [George W.] Bush has stated that bringing bin Laden to justice is just the first step. Over the years ahead, the President and our own Prime Minister [Great Britain's Tony Blair] have effectively sworn to rip out the very roots of terrorism, regardless of international boundaries and, by implication, some cultural sensibilities too. This will represent a very tall order for Western intelligence services. Judging by their performance to date, they have no mindset—not to say stomach—for the sort of HUMINT (human intelligence) operations demanded by such aspirations. The problem for the CIA and, to a lesser extent, our own Secret Intelligence Service (SIS) is a cultural one. Both have been slow to adapt from the rarefied environment of the Cold War. No longer can HUMINT be caricatured as sidling up to the right people at the embassy cocktail party.

The plain truth is that there is no obvious model on which to base our future security structure. There have been many column inches written on the subject. . . . Some have trumpeted a new chapter of the Great Game, cloak-and-dagger antics on the Imperial Frontier: others have demanded a dusting off of the wartime manuals of the Special Operations Executive (SOE). Both have their validity, spanning as they do the twilight zone between classic espionage and the looser end of military operations—the terrorists' own domain. But both veer dangerously towards the romantic, and away from the sheer nastiness of what is now required.

Despite its scale and parochial nature, Northern Ireland is perhaps a better analogy. Our security presence there arguably constitutes the only truly seamless military-intelligence operation in the world at the moment.

> *"The better the intelligence, the better the targeting—and the fewer calls for cumbersome, high-visibility strikes and pointless, showy ground raids."*

It has taken decades to evolve, years to break down the worst of the 'turf' barriers that separate its various agencies and forces. It is, however, now sufficiently established to demonstrate that the better the intelligence, the better the targeting—and the fewer calls for cumbersome, high-visibility strikes and pointless, showy ground raids, which, in this case, will only serve to harden even moderate Muslims against the West.

CIA Intelligence-Gathering Methods Have Been Successful in Fighting Terrorism

by James L. Pavitt

About the author: *James L. Pavitt is the deputy director for operations at the CIA.*

[Editor's Note: The following speech was delivered at the American Bar Association Standing Committee on Law and National Security Breakfast Program on January 23, 2003.]

There is something uniquely American about this gathering. Because only in America would you find the head of the Clandestine Service [the CIA], not only speaking on the record, but speaking on the record in a room filled with lawyers and reporters.

Remember that the next time somebody tries to tell you that the Central Intelligence Agency is risk averse.

In 1942, on a winter morning in neutral Spain, a member of the Office of Strategic Services—our wartime parent—faced one of the hardest decisions of his life. His mission was to take a train through Vichy France to Bern, Switzerland—to slip past the Nazis into the heart of Europe. His timing could not have been worse. That very morning, Allied troops landed in North Africa—triggering a German clampdown on all travelers in France. A difficult task had now become nearly impossible. His choice was stark: he could stay in the safety of Spain or he could brave the Gestapo at the border. He weighed the risks—knowing his life was at stake—and pressed on, using charm and creativity to get into Switzerland. This was no ordinary traveler. His job was to gather intelligence in Bern, intelligence that would prove critical in the fight against Nazi

Germany. That American's name was Allen Dulles. And his career, ranging from operations officer to Director of Central Intelligence, was marked by a passion for espionage, paired with a patriotic determination to succeed. As Director Dulles was fond of saying, "I have never believed in turning back where there is any chance of going forward." I have the honor of leading a group of men and women who have that same passion for espionage and the same patriotic determination to serve their country at a time of great need.

The basic fact of the day is that we meet in extraordinary times. Our nation is at war. And it is a war unlike any other we have ever fought, but a war nonetheless. When an enemy takes more than 3,000 lives on a single morning, [as terrorists did in the attacks of September 11, 2001] you can call it nothing else.

More than two centuries ago, in a clash of wills and weapons stretching over six years, the American military lost in battle some 4,400 men to win our freedom. As great as those sacrifices were, the sacrifices required to preserve our freedom have proven to be vastly greater.

For it is a lesson of history that liberty attracts not only those who wish to prosper in its light, but those determined to snuff it out, those who know that their ideas can prevail only in the darkness of oppression, ignorance, and misery.

Who are these people? The kind of man who would say: "One death is a tragedy, a million deaths is a statistic." The kind of man who would say: "The killing of Jews and Americans is one of the greatest duties."

> *"During the decade of the 1990s . . . the Intelligence Community tripled funding for counter-terrorism."*

The first was [Joseph] Stalin. The second was [terrorist] Usama bin Ladin [who masterminded the September 11 attacks]. And though the circumstances and beliefs that gave rise to each are very different, as are the forces on which each could call, they are in some ways two of a kind.

Though their words are different, their language is the same. It is the language of intolerance and hate and the language of indifference to the suffering and death of innocent men, women, and children.

The agency I represent, and the directorate I am privileged to lead, were born in the early days of the Cold War, the conflict with Stalin and the Soviet Union. But they were not created merely to wage that difficult and that dangerous contest.

They were built to give our country a powerful advantage in its role as a global superpower, a role it still holds today in another conflict with another foe. And it is about that foe—and the demands now imposed on CIA's Directorate of Operations [DO]—that I would like to talk today.

Facing a New Foe

To state a clear principle: We are not at war with a faith, a people, or a part of the globe. What we conveniently call the "Muslim world" is home to more than

1.3 billion human beings with hundreds of languages and cultures. Any student of its rich diversity can find in that huge region both currents of promise and currents of danger.

What you cannot find are massed armies of fanatics, poised to strike at any target of convenience. We are at war with what [Director of Central Intelligence] George Tenet rightly describes as "the fringe of the fringe of the Muslim world." Incredibly committed, incredibly dangerous, but not incredibly numerous.

Their terrible strength lies elsewhere—in their relative anonymity and in their absolute ruthlessness. This we saw so clearly on September 11th.

I am often asked if we, as a nation, could have prevented those terrible attacks. In terms of intelligence, I personally remain convinced that—given what we knew that day—the answer is sadly no. In terms of the bigger picture—the laws and regulations of our land as they were written then—we can ask:

Could the FBI have held men who were in this country legally and who had broken no laws? Was it a crime to take a box cutter aboard a plane?

CIA, along with much of the rest of our government, was no stranger to the terrorist target. We began to work against it in a specific, concerted way in the mid-1980s, when the world was still defined largely by the East-West divide.

Our knowledge grew, as did our successes, through the lean years of the mid-1990s. I would like to take you back there for just a moment.

> *"Great efforts . . . were made at CIA before 9/11 against a very secretive and disciplined enemy."*

What were the realities? In the Intelligence Community as a whole, the number of intelligence positions dropped by almost a quarter. At CIA, recruitment of case officers and all-source analysts—the heart of our organization—came to a virtual halt.

As we shrank, some in Washington spoke hopefully of a "peace dividend," never, never imagining that our enemies would ultimately cash in part of that so-called dividend.

After the bombing of the World Trade Center in 1993, and the successful disruption of a broader operation to destroy key landmarks in New York, we understood that the hands of terror—resolute and resilient—would seek to strike at the United States again and again—here and overseas.

And let's not forget that it was during the decade of the 1990s—when choices and tradeoffs were as hard to make as they have ever been—that the Intelligence Community tripled funding for counter-terrorism. We may have lacked many things in those days, but focus was never one of them.

We kept that powerful focus amid a host of other, competing national security priorities. Some—like Haiti, Bosnia, and Kosovo—have quickly slipped from the front pages. Others—including Korea, the Israeli-Palestinian conflict, and Saddam Hussein's Iraq—are still there.

Chapter 2

My point is that each issue we have to deal with, and there are many more beyond those I have just cited, demand time, attention, people, and dollars. I want to be very clear. That is not a complaint. That is not an excuse. It is, however, a reality. A reality we cannot afford to forget when discussing the health and performance of American intelligence.

When President [Dwight D.] Eisenhower came out to Langley, [Virginia, the location of CIA Headquarters], in November of 1959 to lay the cornerstone of our Headquarters building, he gave voice to a fundamental truth of espionage. "Success," he said, "cannot be advertised. Failure cannot be explained."

In large part, that remains valid today. But one result of the inquiries into the tragedy of September 11th is that the American people have—I believe—a far better sense of what their intelligence agencies can and cannot do. We have now had a chance to share, in general terms, the difficulties we face and the breakthroughs we have made.

We have been able to tell some of our story. It is a story of amazing triumphs—of terrorist assaults averted, of terrorist cells disrupted, of countless innocent lives spared. And is also a story of painful losses—of our embassies in East Africa, of the USS *Cole*, and, most horrible of all, of September 11th itself. I am very conscious of those terrible losses.

The months and years before that unforgettable Tuesday morning were filled with intense, at times even feverish, activity. Working with our partners in this country and overseas, we amassed a great deal of intelligence about Bin Ladin and the global network of murder that we have all come to know as al-Qai'da.

And these were targets we did not simply study. With creativity and daring, we went on the offensive against them.

The men and women who did this work—who sifted patiently and expertly through mountains of incomplete, often contradictory, information to develop leads and make us smarter about a mortal threat, and those who ran the risks out on the streets to take terrorists off them—these unsung heroes performed exceptionally under enormous stress and enormous challenge. Exceptionally, not perfectly. Deep in the last century, Senator Hiram

> *"The primary cause of the [terrorist] attacks was not a memo ignored, a message untranslated, or a name left off a watch list."*

Johnson of California claimed that truth was the first casualty of war. I am not that pessimistic. To me, the first casualty of war is perfection. Not the expectation of perfection—that can be a hardy survivor, and it is, but the reality of perfection.

I think the distinction is important.

I know better than anyone else the great efforts that were made at CIA before 9/11 against a very secretive and disciplined enemy. And I know the great people who made them. But the fact is, despite everything we did, we—and the rest of our government—were unable to uncover the tactical information—the who, where, how, and when—that might have given us a clearer picture of this deadly conspiracy.

It was not, as some have suggested, a simple matter of connecting dots. Could certain things have been done differently? As with most any human enterprise, the answer is yes, of course. What is done well can always be done better.

But, as our country continues its investigation into these brutal terrorist attacks, there is one conclusion we should keep fixed in our minds:

> *"In intelligence . . . a coalition of nations—Muslim and non-Muslim alike—has taken shape to combat the specter of terror."*

The primary cause of the attacks was not a memo ignored, a message untranslated, or a name left off a watch list. Their primary cause was a man named Usama Bin Ladin and a group named al-Qa'ida.

When President George W. Bush decided to strip both Usama Bin Ladin and al-Qai'da of their Afghan sanctuary—a decision that moved the war on terror to an entirely different level—the contribution of intelligence was soon very plain to see. The first American team on the ground out there was CIA—for a reason.

The CIA's Contribution

We had people with the right local languages, we had people with the right local contacts, and the right universal skills—the ability both to report conditions and, if need be, to change them for the better. And they were ready to move, at virtually a moment's notice.

That brand of agile knowledge defines the Directorate of Operations. Its application in Afghanistan gave our military and our allies a priceless edge in their battles with the Taliban and al-Qai'da. In short order, one tyranny was driven from power, its dreams of an endless Dark Age shattered. And a second tyranny was put to flight, its agents scattered after a stunning defeat.

The CIA's contributions in Afghanistan continue to this day. They are possible for one reason: The agency did not, contrary to what you sometimes hear, forget that country, or that region, after the Soviets pulled out in 1989. You simply cannot create overnight the combination of assets—the talent, the sources—that went into the highest possible gear in defense of America after September 11th.

From the wrecked bases of terror, from those captured in Operation Enduring Freedom, we have learned much. Now, with al-Qai'da flushed from its central haven, we are in a long and perilous phase of hunt and pursuit of its cells and sympathizers. And as our president has said to the world, we will find them and we will destroy them.

But let's be clear about this: the task is difficult and the war will be long. As we move and adjust, so do our enemies. They adapt. They regroup. As we have seen in many places, from Bali to North Africa and the waters off Yemen, they retain their ability to strike. And they retain as well their interest in developing and acquiring more gruesome weapons of destruction and fear.

The operational environment may be tough. The possibility of new attacks against us may be high. Yet we as Americans can take some comfort in the fact that we are by no means alone in this campaign. In intelligence, as in military affairs and diplomacy, a coalition of nations—Muslim and non-Muslim alike—has taken shape to combat the specter of terror.

On September 12th, much of the international community—through its intelligence services—came to CIA and asked how they could help. Beyond sympathy, solidarity, or any calculation of gain was an understanding that terrorism threatens more than the United States. In its rage, corruption, and quest for power, it is a threat to governments and peoples everywhere.

The Directorate of Operations has many close and productive liaison relationships. To us, these are force multipliers, valuable extensions of our own activities. With the stakes as high as they are, I would be irresponsible not to use every legitimate resource at my command.

But, fundamentally, for the spies we run, the secrets we steal, and the insights we develop about the world—be it pinpoint events like a terrorist plan or the broader, deeper currents that lie behind them—we rely first and foremost on ourselves and our skills as intelligence professionals.

It has always been so. Today, however, we have more reporting on the really hard targets than I can remember at any time in my nearly 30 years of agency service.

The achievements of the Directorate of Operations—what it brings to the security of the United States each and every day—are the product of the sweat and sacrifice of its people. They are a mix of veteran officers and newer recruits, brought in over the past five years as the leadership of CIA has sought to rebuild the Clandestine Service.

> *"[The CIA is] as aggressive as the law and common sense allow us to be."*

After a period of neglect, when some in government saw little need for our existence, others were giving us more missions, and fewer still thought to give us the money or people to accomplish them, the tide began to turn in 1998. Now, we are hiring at an unprecedented rate. President Bush and Vice President [Dick] Cheney's support for our efforts is unprecedented. Our support from Congress is also unprecedented.

Answering the Critics

There are some misperceptions out there about our recruiting drive. Some claim that we have lowered our standards. One fellow—who once worked at CIA and should know better—said that the officers of today are reluctant to take the hard jobs and reluctant to go to the danger spots of the moment. That's just nonsense!

I want to be very clear: We have plenty of our people posted wherever our mission takes us. The personal risks are enormous; the intelligence gains significant. Those who fear a risk averse Directorate of Operations simply do not know what we are about.

> *"A country that is so tightly closed as to be utterly immune to terrorism is not one I would choose to serve."*

To those critics who were in the past part of the agency, I invite you to put down your coffee, climb out of your armchair, and get back in the fight. For years in the DO, we have had a very successful reserve officer program. If you have what it takes, we welcome your ideas and experience.

I have heard many recommendations from well-meaning observers about the utility of having case officers who know foreign languages, the need to keep human intelligence as our major mission, even the desirability—when no other alternative exists—of bringing on undesirable people as clandestine sources on topics like terrorism, proliferation, and international crime.

Let me say it as clearly as I can: We are doing these things. We have always done these things. We are as aggressive as the law and common sense allow us to be. No one at CIA should fear floating a chancy, but well-thought-out proposal up the chain of command. We live with chance. One of my jobs is to support and encourage those who meet it face-to-face.

And, frankly, timidity has never been much of an issue in the Directorate of Operations. The people within it are just not built that way.

The Quality of CIA Officers

The spirit and skill of the men and women I lead far surpass my powers of description. But to offer even the roughest idea of the patriots drawn to intelligence and espionage, let me take, as an example, the class of Clandestine Service Trainees who graduated [in 2002].

In that group, you would find MBAs, a PhD, and a healthy sprinkling of attorneys, among others. Speakers of Arabic and Korean, among others. Americans of many backgrounds, all willing to pledge their talents to a cause greater than themselves.

Although we are getting more résumés than we have ever gotten, we are as selective as we have ever been. By Washington standards, the Directorate of Operations is very small. But this business has never really been about numbers. Here, agility and flexibility count for much more. And so, we recruit not only for abilities and experience, but for attitude.

We need officers with energy and imagination, ever willing to learn. Officers with a sense of curiosity and adventure, at home in more than one culture. Officers of courage who can take an operational idea, and properly weigh the potential risks against the potential gains. Carrying as we do the reputation of the United States, our aim is to be bold, not reckless.

This is not a calling for everyone. And not everyone selected for training ultimately makes the grade. I expect, indeed demand, a great deal of those in the Clandestine Service, because our nation does as well. The missions with which we are entrusted are some of the most serious and sensitive undertaken anywhere in our government.

A key part of our training—and a key part of our business—centers on responsibility and integrity. Denial and deception we reserve for our targets.

We understand that secrecy is a grant of trust, not a grant of immunity. We understand that we act in the name of the American people, and that we must act in keeping with the laws they honor and the values they cherish.

You should be very proud of the work done by your Directorate of Operations. I certainly am.

Each and every one of us signed up to preserve and protect the Constitution. A country that is so tightly closed as to be utterly immune to terrorism is not one I would choose to serve. In fact, I would not even want to live there.

One of the many things that set us as a people apart from those we fight is the vigorous exchange of ideas. For those of us in the world of intelligence, much of that dialogue must, of necessity, take place behind closed doors. Not just within the Intelligence Community, but between that Community and the people's representatives—the oversight committees of Congress.

It is a rare privilege for me to get out and meet with an audience like this. Together, we are in a new age. An age of hazard. An age captured in the creation of a Department of Homeland Security—a development few Americans could have foreseen even a few short years ago. We are in the midst of one war, with a second a distinct possibility.

With all those things in mind—which limit what I can say—I would very much like to hear from you. Your thoughts. Your questions. Your concerns.

But first, let me thank you for your attention and the warm welcome you afforded me here this morning. Thank you.

Counterespionage Reforms at U.S. Intelligence Agencies Are Unnecessary

by Jay Taylor

About the author: *Jay Taylor was deputy assistant secretary of state for intelligence coordination during the Ronald Reagan administration.*

Fear of foreign spies was already inordinately high in the United States when the sensational espionage charges against [FBI agent] Robert Philip Hanssen hit the headlines. The media and the public, always starved for drama, have been captivated. The executive branch is planning tough-sounding remedies, including new super organizations. Existing counterintelligence bureaucracies have exploited the "crisis" to grow and expand. And counterspy measures, resources and personnel are already greater than they were during the height of the Cold War.

President [George W.] Bush is expected soon to approve establishment of a new counterintelligence policy board headed by a counterintelligence czar who will report to a new counterintelligence board of directors. This, despite the fact that there is no more KGB, [the intelligence agency of the former Soviet Union], no more Soviet Union.

Judging by discussions in the media, the new so-called proactive measures being planned are those that monitor our own people and control sensitive documents. An example of one of these measures is the explosion in job opportunities for internal security agents in the State Department. If former Secretary of State Madeleine Albright's plan is carried out, State will hire 500 new security agents, bringing the total of such officers in the foreign service to 1,500. This compares with a total of only 2,500 foreign service officers who perform the department's core work of diplomacy—reporting, analysis, advocacy and negotiation on bilateral and international issues—including ambassadors, their deputies and other program direction officers.

While security expands, some 700 other foreign service positions remain vacant because of lack of funding. Some of the work normally done by diplomats is now being performed by officers in our foreign missions from the CIA and the Pentagon, neither of which have a comparable budget problem.

An Exaggerated Threat

Yet the current danger we face from foreign espionage is a mere fraction of that posed from the 1930s to the fall of the Soviet Union in 1991. The mighty KGB's successor, the SVR, like the Soviet Navy and all the other wings of the old Communist regime's security establishment, is a shadow of its former self. For eight years, the SVR did not even contact Hanssen, one of the best-positioned moles in the United States the old KGB ever had. Except for Cuba, the SVR has lost all of the KGB's sister services, including the once extraordinarily effective East German Stasi. Moreover, since the emergence of Russia as a relatively open but very strained society, the ability of Western services to penetrate the SVR has geometrically increased. The double agent in the SVR who exposed the apparent double-crosser Hanssen apparently handed over the entire KGB file.

The deeds of our counterspy turncoats resulted in the deaths of some of our Russian moles and are deserving of harsh punishment, but the consequences of their actions had no critical impact on vital U.S. interests. Notably, the FBI tunnel under the Russian Embassy in Washington reportedly revealed by Hanssen apparently produced no major intelligence. (Likewise the previous big American tunneling exercise, the famous 1950s CIA dig in Berlin, was a bust from the start. A Russian mole in London tipped off the KGB to the project before it even began.)

To declare to the press, as some intelligence sources are doing, that Hanssen and [CIA mole] Aldrich Ames brought about the "greatest losses in the history of American intelligence" is to focus on damage to the counterspy organizations themselves and not to basic national interests, as for example was the case in the theft of nuclear secrets or submarine codes.

The massive spying and internal security apparatus of the KGB did not save the Soviet Union. Why now, when we face no such monolithic monster, do we need a counterintelligence czar, expanded polygraphs, more intrusive monitoring of personnel, a draconian "official secrets act" and many more internal security agents in the State Department and elsewhere?

We won the hot and cold wars the old way, by maintaining a reasonable level of internal controls but concentrating on offense—penetration, mole implantation and communications intercepts. We need to safeguard counterintelligence and other sensitive information, but the possibilities and the consequences of both foreign espionage and counterspying should be kept in perspective.

As George F. Kennan, architect of America's Cold War containment policy, once observed, counterintelligence takes on aspects that cause it to be viewed as a game, played in its own right. The fascination it exerts, he concluded, tends wholly to obscure, even for the general public, the original reasons for it.

The CIA Should Not Become Involved in Direct Combat Operations

by Bruce Berkowitz

About the author: *Bruce Berkowitz is a research fellow at the Hoover Institution, a public policy research center devoted to advanced study in domestic public policy and international affairs.*

Nine days after the September 11, 2001, terrorist strikes on New York and Washington [DC], George W. Bush explained to the country how the government planned to respond. Speaking on prime-time television before a joint session of Congress, he described the coming war: "Our response involves far more than instant retaliation and isolated strikes. Americans should not expect one battle, but a lengthy campaign, unlike any other we have ever seen. It may include dramatic strikes visible on TV and covert operations secret even in success."

President Bush was almost certainly speaking from a text scrutinized by the White House staff, members of a half-dozen cabinet departments, and echelons of lawyers. Thus *covert operations* was a carefully chosen phrase.

Never before has a president announced so explicitly that covert operations would be a major part of U.S. policy. His announcement is a direct result of the new kind of threat we face: global terrorist organizations. Having raised the issue, we need to consider whether, where, and when to use covert action to fight terrorism.

Of the four basic options for dealing with foreign terrorist threats, each is appropriate for a different set of conditions.

Examining the Options

The first option is diplomacy and cooperation with foreign law enforcement agencies. This works when a country has a functioning government and operates in good faith with the United States. The [Bill] Clinton administration, unfortunately, relied on cooperation even when a government was clearly unwilling or unable to work with us, with the result that terrorists had more territory from which to operate safely. The reluctance of Saudi Arabia to cooperate with the United States in the Khobar Towers bombing investigation was one example. Yemen's foot-dragging behavior after the attack on the USS *Cole* was another.

The second option is full-scale war against countries that willfully harbor terrorists. This was the case in Afghanistan. Al Qaeda had virtually taken over the government, as it was the main bankroller of the Taliban regime. When U.S. officials linked Al Qaeda to the September 11 attacks, the Taliban refused to turn over its "guests." Given the evidence and the Taliban's clear lack of cooperation, it was easy for the United States to justify military action under international law, which allows armed self-defense. But terrorist organizations, learning from the experience of Al Qaeda, will likely avoid providing the United States a clear justification for full-scale war.

> *"All military force should be overt—openly linked to the U.S. government."*

Also, full-scale war usually requires the support of allies. Even when the United States is willing to do most of the fighting, we still need allies to provide bases, airspace, and intelligence. If one does not have such support, full-scale military operations are difficult or impossible.

In the future, then, terrorist organizations will be more careful in choosing where to set up shop. Most likely, they will pick countries that are not quite enemies of the United States but certainly not friends either. They could choose countries with governments not fully in control. Combined with terrorists' efforts to hide and disavow responsibility for their actions, the United States could have an increasingly difficult time finding allies willing to support full-scale, overt military operations—even when the United States can claim grounds for armed self-defense. The third and fourth options—covert action and direct action—are discussed below.

Using Covert Action

The legal definition of covert action appears in the U.S. Code (Title 50, Chapter 15, Section 413b), which defines *covert action* as any "activity or activities of the United States Government to influence political, economic, or military conditions abroad, where it is intended that the role of the United States Government will not be apparent or acknowledged publicly." In other words, covert actions are deniable activities.

It is telling that the main reason for defining covert action in the law has been to establish procedures for approving such activities and notifying Congress. Covert operations hide the visible signs of U.S. responsibility. Thus we need special provisions to maintain control, oversight, and accountability through other—classified—channels.

It is important to understand that covert operations are not secret operations. Secret operations are supposed to be concealed completely from the public. Some high-tech weapons, for example, are secret. By hiding them, we prevent enemies from developing countermeasures. Some diplomacy is secret, too, allowing U.S. officials greater flexibility in floating ideas or negotiating the early stages of an agreement free from public pressure.

Most covert operations are, in contrast, entirely visible. The only thing secret about these activities is the U.S. role. Indeed, almost anything the United States has done as a covert action—paramilitary operations, security assistance, and so on—has been done overtly on other occasions. Thus the first questions to ask about any proposed covert operation are "Why do you want to do it covertly?" and "Why is concealing the role of the U.S. government essential to its success?"

Usually, the only good reason for covertness is that public knowledge of U.S. responsibility would make the operation much less effective or simply impossible to carry out. For instance, some propaganda will have a greater impact on foreign audiences if it seems to come from a neutral source. Payoffs or security protection to a foreign official could discredit the official or give his rivals political ammunition if they became public.

Which brings us to combating terrorism. Sometimes direct, open involvement with the United States might make it impossible for an otherwise willing foreign government to cooperate with us. For example, the press has reported that teams from the Department of Defense (DOD) and the CIA are helping Pakistan and the Philippines in tracking Al Qaeda cells. The United States has had "complicated" relations with these countries in the past—another way of saying we supported military dictators in both countries during the 1970s and 1980s as part of our Cold War efforts to contain the Soviet Union—which is why we now need to reduce the visibility of U.S. support. In the Philippines, a large U.S. presence would be burdensome political baggage for the current government (a democracy installed with U.S. assistance in 1986). In Pakistan, a visible U.S. presence could be a rallying cry for religious fundamentalists who oppose the current regime. General Pervez Musharraf may have come to power via a coup, but he has at least declared his intentions of building democracy. The fundamentalists want a theocratic state.

> *"When U.S. forces fight covertly . . . our combat operations begin to resemble those of terrorists."*

Keeping Distinctions Clear

Even so, there are situations in which U.S. leaders might be tempted to use covert action to fight terrorists but should not. The rule of thumb should be whether the United States plans to send armed forces into combat. Simply put, *all* military force should be overt—openly linked to the U.S. government.

We must keep clear distinctions between terrorists and ourselves. Regular armies and terrorists often fight using similar methods—small, semi-autonomous cells dispersed over vast regions. This is simply the nature of modern warfare; any army that fights in large, pre-set formations is vulnerable, and modern communication networks make it possible for combat forces to operate as small, highly mobile units. Terrorists have access to the same technology and are using similar tactics.

The main differences between terrorists and regular armies are the rules they follow when they fight. Uniformed military forces are an expression of every nation's legitimate right of self-defense. In principle, they are trained to operate under international rules of war. Under these rules, they try to avoid killing noncombatants. Just as important, they identify themselves openly when they fight by wearing uniforms or insignia. This lets them distinguish themselves from noncombatants and makes their governments responsible for their actions. Terrorists, in contrast, do not abide by the rules of war. They target noncombatants to create fear and confusion. That is, after all, the definition of terror. Terrorists also hide their identities. This makes it harder to find them and harder to hold their sponsors responsible for their actions. It also makes it harder to fight them without harming noncombatants.

This is why using covert action to fight terrorists presents problems. When U.S. forces fight covertly—that is, when they hide U.S. responsibility by not wearing insignia or reporting through a clear, public chain of command—our combat operations begin to resemble those of terrorists. This undermines the credibility and moral standing of the United States.

Choosing Direct Action

Another option for using lethal force against terrorists is direct action. This kind of activity has received much less attention than covert action in the past but is likely to be more important in the future.

The DOD *Dictionary of Military and Associated Terms* defines *direct action* as "short-duration strikes and other small-scale offensive actions by special operations forces or special operations-capable units to seize, destroy, capture, recover, or inflict damage on designated personnel or materiel." Strip away the jargon, and you are talking about ambushing terrorist groups, raiding weapons shipments in transit, and rescuing hostages. Direct action is not a show of force. It is military force to achieve important, but limited, objectives.

A key difference between direct action and covert action is that in direct action the United States does not conceal its responsibility. Soldiers wear uniforms and insignia, which is an important difference between a covert paramilitary operation and direct action. Direct action involves innovative military action to eliminate terrorists—while not acting like terrorists ourselves.

Besides complying with international law, direct action has another advantage over covert military operations. It compels presidents to acknowledge that undertaking combat is an act of war and forces them to decide whether they can justify that step and whether they want to take it.

Finally, because U.S. responsibility for direct action is public, politicians have no place to hide if things go sour. Planners of operations, because they are under greater public scrutiny, are more likely to learn from their mistakes. Recall the failed 1980 U.S. hostage rescue mission in Iran. Because it was not covert, the [Jimmy] Carter administration had to take responsibility (which, admirably, it did). The U.S. military learned that it was not prepared and the public understood this. As a result, military officials proposed fixes and Congress supported them.

> *"If the CIA starts to fight wars, it will be less able to conduct espionage."*

Are We Prepared?

Ironically, many military officers who would be responsible for direct action have been skeptical about using it. General Henry Shelton, while chairman of the Joint Chiefs of Staff and himself a member of the army's Special Forces, supposedly once derided such operations as "going Hollywood." In fairness, they do conjure up visions of Mr. T and *The A-Team* or Napoleon Solo and *The Man from U.N.C.L.E.*

But we will likely require this capability in the war on terrorism. The new threat demands it. Moreover, to carry out direct action effectively, we will need to develop new capabilities. We currently lack the ability to react quickly. Logistics support is also a problem.

Currently, U.S. Special Operations forces can move faster than, say, an army division or a navy carrier battle group. Even so, deploying a special operations force of almost any kind remains a big military operation. Putting almost any combat unit into the field still requires days—even weeks—to prepare. Also, the DOD lacks effective means of supporting small units in the field once they are deployed. This is why the CIA—rather than the DOD—put the first U.S. combat forces into Afghanistan after September 11. It was not because we needed to be covert; the whole world knew we were at war. It was just that the CIA could move faster, using its network of case officers, contractors, and cooperating foreign governments.

But using the CIA as a quick-response arm of the DOD is a bad idea. Few organizations do more than one thing well. If the CIA starts to fight wars, it will be less able to conduct espionage—that is, recruit spies, perform analysis, and support noncombat covert operations. Consider how much has been revealed about the CIA's activities in Afghanistan. The press carried reports about the CIA's military assistance teams even before it learned what the DOD was doing in Afghanistan. Can any organization with this kind of visibility operate secretly? The press also reported that the CIA operated Predator unmanned aircraft to track Taliban units and attack them with missiles. If the CIA did this while trying to maintain deniability, then it was coming dangerously close to re-sembling the terrorists it was trying to destroy.

Preparing the Military

It makes more sense to better prepare U.S. military forces for direct action. The defense department must develop small, highly mobile combat forces to at-tack the new threats we face. It must also develop the specialized infrastructure it needs for logistics, communications, and supplies.

Direct action is overt military force, but such operations may require covert ac-tivities for support. For example, if a terrorist organization takes refuge in a country that is surrounded by countries hostile to the United States, there may be nowhere in the neighborhood for a U.S. staging area. In such a case, the United States may need to set up bases covertly before the operation. This might seem like a role for the CIA, but, again, there are good reasons it should not be di-rectly involved. Any military operation that used the CIA's secret infrastructure would likely compromise the agency's spying operations. The last thing you want to do if you are trying to maintain safe houses and dead drops is to call at-tention to yourself with helicopters, armored vehicles, and people in fa-tigues carrying automatic weapons.

> *"Let spies be spies and soldiers be soldiers."*

The DOD must develop this capa-bility itself. The laws that define oversight requirements for CIA covert action also allow the DOD to carry out similar operations to support combat operations. For example, the Title 50 re-quirements for notifying Congress about covert operations exclude "traditional military operations"—including direct actions and the clandestine activities needed to support them. These activities are authorized under different laws and have their own notification requirements. By starting afresh, the military ser-vices could also explore new approaches to providing cover and operating a covert infrastructure.

Let spies be spies and soldiers be soldiers. We will need them both.

Dealing with terrorism—as well as similar asymmetric threats—will require diplomacy, law enforcement, and a range of military capabilities. This choice will depend partly on the nature of the threat—small power, great power, or something in between—and whether we can count on the support of allies. It will also depend on whether we can use the rule of law or must resort to force.

The long-range goal of the United States should be to promote cooperative, democratic governments so that diplomacy and cooperative law enforcement are effective in as much of the world as possible. In the meantime, the most im-portant ingredient in dealing with terrorism will be leaders who can make ex-plicit, high-level decisions about which combination of capabilities is most ap-propriate in each case.

Tighter Controls to Prevent Espionage at U.S. Research Laboratories Are Harmful

by Neal Lane

About the author: *Neal Lane, former assistant for science and technology to President Bill Clinton, is a university professor and senior fellow at the James A. Baker III Institute for Public Policy at Rice University, in Houston, Texas.*

A foreign graduate student at a major U.S. university developed a new hybrid rocket fuel. A U.S. company wanted to fund further testing, but insisted it could not even discuss it unless the university obtained an export license. Repeated in countless variations, this kind of episode crystallizes the conflict that the United States faces between two competing objectives: How to protect U.S. national security while deepening the cooperation with the international scientific community that is essential for both U.S. prosperity and security.

Balancing Conflicting Objectives

Balancing these objectives is not new and has only become more imperative since the end of the Cold War. But, prompted by such events as the Wien Ho Lee espionage case[1] the U.S. Congress has pushed for fighter controls on foreign researchers seeking access to U.S. scientists, technologies, and facilities— a move that threatens to shift the balance between openness and security controls in the wrong direction. Unless the . . . [George W. Bush] administration recognizes the importance of this issue and reduces impediments to international exchange, major areas of U.S. science and technology will suffer badly.

Although today's security environment differs markedly from the situation during the era of superpower rivalry, the issue of scientific communication and its effect on national security was just as relevant then as it is now. In 1981,

---

1. Claims that Lee, a Taiwanese-American scientist, downloaded nuclear weapons data and gave it to the Chinese government were never proven.

presidents of five leading U.S. research universities wrote to the secretaries of state, defense, and commerce to warn of damage inflicted on U.S. science by a new batch of proposed controls on the dissemination of research—in particular, cutting-edge microelectronics. Largely in response to these concerns, U.S. President Ronald Reagan issued National Security Decision Directive 189, which states that "to the maximum extent possible, the products of fundamental research [are to] remain unrestricted." Thus, at the height of the Cold War, an administration that was greatly concerned about preventing adversaries from eroding the U.S. technological advantage affirmed that the free exchange of ideas was so important that it justified the risk that U.S. adversaries might receive some advantages as well.

Today, controls over fundamental research are even less appropriate than they were during the Cold War. At that time, U.S. technology controls were used to buy time, preserve the U.S. lead, and keep adversaries from exploiting the latest technological developments. The task today is differ-

> *"Unless the . . . [George W. Bush] administration . . . reduces impediments to international exchange, major areas of U.S. science and technology will suffer badly."*

ent: The goal is not to prevent competitors from reaching current U.S. standards. Instead, in large measure the most important task is to keep countries of concern such as Iraq and North Korea from catching up to, say, 1945, or maybe to 1960—a harder task, but one for which controls over fundamental research are even less well suited. At the same time, the speed of scientific and technological innovation, the increasing rate at which ideas from one area are stimulating advances in another, and the global disseminating power of the information revolution make international openness necessary for the health of U.S. science and technology. After all, the United States is not ahead in all technical areas.

The Effects of Tighter Controls

The struggle between openness in scientific research and controls in the name of national security has become especially evident in satellite research. Because military and research satellites share common technologies, all satellites are subject to the International Traffic in Arms Regulations (ITAR), which govern U.S. munitions exports. While ITAR does not restrict the reporting of fundamental research results, it governs the unclassified design, manufacture, and use of satellite and booster technologies needed for satellite-based research. . . .

Several events—including criminal prosecutions arising from information divulged to the Chinese in the course of investigations of failed Chinese launches of U.S. satellites—prompted a tightening of satellite export-control regulations, particularly for communications and scientific satellites. As a result, ITAR licensing procedures are delaying and inhibiting collaboration with foreign research groups, slowing international projects like development of the next-generation replacement for the Hubble Space Telescope and a future gamma ray telescope. Moreover, ITAR restrictions put universities conducting space-based research in a very difficult position, requiring them to secure licenses before satellite makers will provide needed, unclassified information to foreign students and faculty. Some universities are threatening to give up satellite-based research before they will make such citizenship-based distinctions.

ITAR also undermines the much larger commercial market. Before U.S. satellite export controls were tightened about two years ago, the U.S. satellite industry won about 70 percent of all international contracts for communications satellites. Today, U.S. export controls have proven so onerous that foreign customers avoid them entirely by eschewing U.S. manufacturers and eliminating the use of U.S. components. The U.S. market share is now about 40 percent and falling, and the extra business no doubt helps foreign providers master the very technologies the United States is trying to protect.

The balancing act between scientific openness and national security is also being tested at the U.S. Department of Energy's nuclear weapons laboratories. Sensational allegations of Chinese espionage and lax security, heated media coverage, and congressional action—best described as "ready, fire, arm"—resulted in more than two dozen new measures, including more lie-detector tests and tightened restrictions on travel and visitor access.

How might a foreign enemy go about attacking the U.S. national security technology base? A particularly insidious adversary might try to destroy morale at U.S. labs, hamstring them with new regulations, isolate them from the international community, drive away their most experienced, knowledgeable workers, and cut them off from promising new hires. It is sobering to consider that we could end up doing this to ourselves. Policymakers must learn to consider security, comprehensively. One at a time, regulations can seem quite reasonable. Put together, they can be self-defeating.

The dangers of new technology-based threats such as cyberattack and bioterrorism are creating pressures to restrict scientific engagement further. But discoveries and inventions are made in every part of the world. The United States benefits far more than it loses from open scientific communication. To

> *"The United States benefits far more than it loses from open scientific communication."*

argue that we should build walls around our labs and our country is to promote a return to some imagined Cold War isolation that in fact never really existed—at least in science. By working with scientists themselves, the Bush administration has an opportunity to prevent that from happening and to ensure a proper balance between scientific cooperation and security controls.

Creating a Defense Department Intelligence Czar Could Bias Intelligence Gathering

by Jason Vest

About the author: *Jason Vest, who writes on national security issues, is a contributing editor to the* Nation.

As the civil liberties community endeavors to stem the tide of threats to the Constitution posed by [Attorney General] John Ashcroft's Justice Department and new Department of Homeland Security, some in Washington policy-making circles watched with trepidation on November 13, 2002, as Congress gave Defense Secretary Donald Rumsfeld permission to create a new Under Secretariat for Intelligence at the Pentagon. According to some observers, not only does the move have the potential to obscure Congressional oversight of much of the nation's intelligence apparatus, but it could result in analysis increasingly politicized and slanted toward reporting what the most hawkish officials want to hear.

To be sure, some observers see the change as nothing more than a simple but long-overdue bureaucratic reform; in fact, it was originally conceived as a kind of "reinventing government" idea under the Clinton Administration. In this view, it's simply an attempt to bring order to the organizational and budgetary chaos of the myriad intelligence agencies that operate under the Defense Department's aegis—from high-tech-oriented outfits like the National Security Agency and National Reconnaissance Office to the specialized intelligence units of each uniformed service. One popular Pentagon anecdote attributes the move to Rumsfeld's frustration at having representatives from nearly a dozen different military intelligence organizations in his office at the same time during the EP-3 spy-plane crisis in China: "All I want is one dog to kick," he reportedly said, angrily noting that instead of one dog, "right now I have a whole kennel."

A Troubling Plan

Yet to others, there's much more—and much more that's troubling—to the creation of a Pentagon "intelligence czar." Some veterans of the national security establishment see it as part of the Administration hawks' plan to institutionalize a serious counterbalance to the CIA, which has not produced the analysis the hawks want to hear: namely, that there are real, substantial links between [Iraqi leader] Saddam Hussein and Osama bin Laden [the terrorist who masterminded the September 11, 2001, attacks]. "This is basically showing the following: If you don't get the intelligence you want, you create something that will give it to you," says Mel Goodman, a former senior CIA analyst who now teaches at the National War College.

> *"[Creating] an Under Secretariat for Intelligence at the Pentagon . . . could result in analysis increasingly politicized and slanted."*

Indeed, the idea of a Pentagon intelligence czar is 180 degrees from the recommendation of another [George W.] Bush Administration official, retired Lieutenant General Brent Scowcroft, who was National Security Adviser under the first Bush Administration and now serves the younger Bush as chair of the President's Foreign Intelligence Advisory Board. In his capacity as chair of a special commission on intelligence reform, in March [2002] Scowcroft recommended that several key intelligence functions now run and funded under military authority be transferred to civilian control. While George Tenet, the Director of Central Intelligence (DCI), technically coordinates the entire intelligence community, he has both operational and budgetary control only over the CIA. Scowcroft's recommendation was to separate the traditionally dual role of the DCI, making one person DCI with coordinating responsibility for all US government intelligence functions (commonly called the Intelligence Community, IC), one person director of the CIA, and moving the National Security Agency, National Reconnaissance Office and National Imagery and Mapping Agency to independent-agency status under the new DCI.

Rumsfeld and his longtime cohort in all things hawkish, Vice President Dick Cheney, didn't take too kindly to Scowcroft's recommendation. In the milieu of Washington, where the size of the budget one controls is a source of power, the loss of such big-ticket agencies would not only diminish the Defense Department's clout but remove from its control some of the most valued collectors of sensitive information—which, for the hawks' agenda, are quite important.

Control Without Oversight

The Congressional authorization not only effectively neuters Scowcroft's recommendations, says a veteran of the CIA's Directorate of Operations; it also creates the potential for covert operations under Pentagon control that have no oversight. "Covert operations," he notes, "are generally done through the CIA, and the requirements are presidential authorization and then notification of the Gang of Eight—the chairs and ranking minority members of the Congressional intelligence committees and the majority and minority leaders of both houses." Some in the intelligence community are now wondering whether, in addition to going to the Pentagon for the analysis it wants to hear, the White House might task the new Pentagon intelligence office with certain covert operations that might not be shared in an expeditious or complete manner—if at all—with the DCI or Congress.

Intelligence scholar and National Security Archives senior fellow Jeffrey Richelson echoes these concerns, noting the lack of debate and clarity on just what the new under secretary's role will be. "If the job's role is to manage the Pentagon intelligence agencies for the Secretary of Defense and the Director of Central Intelligence better than anyone else has been able to do, it's all for the good," he says. "But if the under secretary tries to be an 'intelligence czar' in some sense trying to compete with or displace the DCI in running these agencies not for overall national security purposes but for DoD purposes, that's not a good thing."

Troubling as this lack of certainty and clarity is, in the context of the current Administration, it's about par for the course. Given that it has done everything from dispatching former DCI (and fellow Iraqophobe) James Woolsey on a comically secret mission to Wales . . . in search of the

> *"The Congressional authorization [of a new office] . . . creates the potential for covert operations under Pentagon control that have no oversight."*

Holy Grail—a link between Saddam and Al Qaeda—to setting up an ad hoc collection-and-analysis operation designed to facilitate the conclusions and actions it wants on Iraq, it's reasonable to puzzle over just what the new directorate is about. Discerning an answer is also difficult, given the unique nature and background of the man likely to become the new under secretary, Richard Haver.

Questioning the Loyalties of the New Leader

A former naval aviator who flew reconnaissance missions in Vietnam, Haver went on reserve status in the early 1970s and returned to the Navy as a civilian analyst. A protégé of William Studeman, a prominent naval intelligence officer who would later make admiral and go on to head the National Security Agency, Haver is almost universally praised for his analytical prowess and "is a straight shooter who won't modify what is true for political reasons," says David Major, a former FBI counterintelligence specialist who has worked with Haver for years. A longtime CIA colleague and ally describes him as "solidly Republican but not an ideologue, and he has a quick mind and gives great advice." On the other hand, the colleague says, "he also tends to talk a lot more than he listens—a style that did not make him an appreciated figure at Langley [Virginia, the location of CIA headquarters]—and he does have strongly held opinions."

As a naval intelligence analyst, Haver headed the damage assessment probe in the 1985 John Walker espionage case, and then was seconded to Langley as chief of the IC management staff. Based on his experience with the Walker damage assessment, Haver ended up directing the Aldrich Ames [spy case] assessment—and, say multiple intelligence community sources, unnecessarily alienating and even mining the careers of some case officers. "I am not going to be an apologist for the agency and say some heads did not need to roll," says a former senior CIA official. But, he and others add, Haver seemed to regard everyone involved in the Ames case—including veteran counterintelligence officer Paul Redmond, who pushed a recalcitrant CIA to start looking for the mole in its midst—as a bad actor, and he "is not someone who inspires warm and cozy feelings at the agency to this day."

Despite his ostensibly nonideological reputation, some in the intelligence community have begun to wonder . . . if this might not be the case any longer. That he first intersected with Rumsfeld as the IC liaison to Rumsfeld's ballistic missile commission has given pause to some; that he was floated as a possible chief for all Pentagon space-warfare issues raises eyebrows as well. . . . Hawks were making little secret of their view (as well as their efforts) that Haver would be the "ideal replacement," as one put it, for George Tenet. And a favorite Haver mantra—"a lack of evidence is not evidence of absence of evidence"—likely puts him in good stead with the hawks on Iraq and other issues. But even Haver's biggest boosters say that while he's a great analyst and adviser, "he has never been a particularly sterling manager," as one puts it. "If the under secretary's job is merely a policy role, pulling together and coordinating budgets, maybe. But beyond that, I'd worry."

Chapter 3

Do Espionage and Intelligence-Gathering Activities Violate Civil Liberties?

Chapter Preface

After the terrorist attacks of September 11, 2001, President George W. Bush declared a war on terrorism. The nation's intelligence agencies immediately implemented national security policies designed to prevent future terrorist attacks against the United States. Some policies expanded these agencies' power to gather intelligence, giving them greater authority to conduct surveillance on, gather information about, and detain individuals suspected of plotting terrorist acts. Shortly thereafter, civil libertarians challenged these policies, renewing the debate over how to balance national security and civil liberties.

Those who support new intelligence-gathering policies argue that preventing the loss of American lives requires some restriction of civil liberties. The United States, they argue, has a history of restricting civil liberties during times of war without experiencing any long-term ill effects. Some claim that the new security policies employed in the war against terrorism pale in comparison to the policies of previous wartime administrations. For example, when the United States feared war with France during John Adams's administration, French refugees, once welcomed, were viewed as potential spies. In consequence, in 1798 Congress passed the Alien and Sedition Acts, which gave the president the power to imprison or deport aliens suspected of activities posing a threat to the national government. During World War I, Woodrow Wilson's administration was successful in inducing Congress to pass the Espionage Act, the Trading with the Enemy Act, and the Sabotage and Sedition Acts, which gave the government power to censor publications and international communications and to punish any expression of opinion considered "disloyal, profane, scurrilous or abusive." During World War II, Franklin Roosevelt signed Executive Order 9066, which authorized the internment of Japanese Americans despite the fact that Roosevelt's intelligence services determined that few of these citizens posed any risk. Author Jay Wink asserts that "despite these previous and numerous extreme measures, there was little long-term or corrosive effect on society after the security threat had subsided. When the crisis ended, normalcy returned and so too did civil liberties, invariably stronger than before."

Some commentators, however, are concerned that the war on terrorism is different from traditional wars and thus requires that government officials exercise special care to maintain civil liberties. Columnist Maggie Gallagher writes, "A war on terrorism, unlike World War II or other U.S. wars, appears to have no fixed enemy and no clear termination date." While these analysts agree that wartime requires the expansion of powers to protect Americans, they want to know whether the United States would ever be able to declare victory in this war. With the conflict so open-ended, they are concerned that newly granted intelligence-gathering powers would be exercised indefinitely.

Some commentators take issue with the expansion of powers during any kind of conflict. According to Ralph G. Neas of People for the American Way, a civil liberties organization, "We have a long history of overreacting during times of crisis. . . . After a while, we usually look back on those actions and realize that they were a mistake, and I think that's what will happen here."

Whether past precedents during times of war justifies Bush's decision to grant intelligence agencies more power to fight terrorism remains controversial. The authors in the following chapter express their opinions on whether civil liberties are threatened by intelligence-gathering activities.

Granting Intelligence Agencies Increased Powers to Fight Terrorism Threatens Civil Liberties

by Philip B. Heymann

About the author: *Philip B. Heymann, former deputy attorney general, is a professor of law at Harvard Law School and the author of* Terrorism and America.

Although much of the concern over managing the tension between liberty and security in response to the . . . terrorist attacks of [September 11, 2001], has been focused on the anti-terrorism bills and the resulting USA Patriot Act (Patriot Act) adopted in late fall 2001, the issues presented by the new statute are less significant than the civil liberties issues resting entirely within the discretion of the executive branch. If the focus of current concern remains centered on the Patriot Act, a number of questions of major importance are likely to escape careful attention and analysis.

The Trade-Offs

The critical trade-offs facing Americans following September 11, arise primarily from choices that must be made among the uses of discretionary powers and the tactical interplay of rules for U.S. citizens with rules for noncitizens rather than from the pitting of rights of Americans to be free of intrusive government action against new powers granted in the name of national security. The critical trade-offs are as follows:

- Privacy rights impacted by the collection and use of information from a wide variety of sources weighed against privacy rights compromised by intrusive investigative techniques;

- Costs in terms of privacy and efficiency of investigating all possible suspects weighed against discriminatory effects of focusing investigation and other preventive steps on groups characterized by specific ethnic characteristics or noncitizenship;
- Internal security measures versus law enforcement measures and the use of intelligence agencies versus law enforcement agencies in fighting terrorism;
- Difficulty of conducting trials in the United States versus assassination abroad or military tribunals (which are spared the problems of open proof and an independent fact finder);
- Greatly increasing the level of intrusiveness of investigative activity in the United States versus encouraging other nations to increase the intrusiveness of their own investigations.

This article will discuss refocusing the powers long available to U.S. law enforcement and intelligence agencies, rather than new statutory powers. The discussion is structured around the risks to American civil liberties (and to the human rights of others) that result from our efforts to increase our security and freedom from fear in three ways—prevention, consequence management, and punishment.

The Efforts to Increase Security

Prevention: We must try to increase our security against major terrorist attacks by some mix of the following preventive measures: (1) learning of a terrorist group's plans in advance, monitoring its efforts, and frustrating those efforts; (2) denying all those who fail some test of loyalty access to targets or the resources needed to attack those targets; (3) combining methods (1) and (2), first monitoring efforts to obtain access to targets and dangerous resources and then monitoring those exerting such efforts; or (4) detaining without criminal conviction those who are most likely to be supportive of an act of terrorism.

Consequence Management: If we fail to prevent a terrorist attack, we must be prepared to minimize its harmful consequences. In the case of massive attacks like those on September 11, or those that might follow from the use of biological or nuclear weapons, consequence management requires the availability of emergency powers that are not generally granted to law enforcement, military, or intelligence agents—a grant that carries with it grave dangers.

> *"The issues presented by the [anti-terrorism bills] are less significant than the civil liberties issues resting entirely within the discretion of the executive branch."*

Punishment: Finally, if we fail to prevent a massive terrorist attack, we in all likelihood will want to retaliate against the terrorists, their leaders, and any states that support the terrorists. Our drive to retaliate, and the forms that this retaliation may take, also raise difficult human rights issues.

The Risks to Privacy and Liberty

Prevention. The safest and surest way of preventing a terrorist attack is to monitor the activities of every individual or group who may even possibly be planning such an attack. Not only would such monitoring be prohibitively expensive, it would expose large numbers of innocent individuals and groups to surveillance because of some small possibility that they could present a danger. The danger of such broad monitoring of law-abiding citizens depends, in part, on how coercive or intrusive the monitoring is, although any monitoring will be intrusive to some extent. The administration's program of requesting interviews from thousands of visiting aliens, without arresting them, for example, is unavoidably coercive because of the vast discretionary powers of the Immigration and Naturalization Service (INS). Noncitizens subject to questioning cannot feel free to refuse to answer.

The use of informants, even if not accompanied by secret searches or electronic surveillance, is likely to create a substantial inhibition of speech and a chilling effect on democratic political activity. To avoid this, recent attorneys general have required in published FBI guidelines that the government have a reasonable suspicion that an individual or group is planning violence or acting on behalf of a foreign power or group to further international terrorism, before authorizing any intelligence gathering to prevent terrorism. Although the required predicate has always been somewhat elastic, in

> *"The use of informants . . . is likely to create a substantial inhibition of speech and a chilling effect on democratic political activity."*

times of crisis it will be stretched to the limit to permit monitoring of any groups that vocally support a state or group engaged in terrorism. Such speech is one of the most important, although one of the weakest, open signs that a person is more likely than others to be engaged in terrorist activities. But even this protection—historically respected by attorneys general, requiring reasonable suspicion of actually planning political violence, is unlikely to survive after the events of September 11, and, indeed, is being reconsidered.

Restricting Access to Targets and Resources. A second form of prevention is to deny a certain class of people access to targets or to the resources needed to attack the targets, e.g., denying access to the plane and fuel tank that could be used to attack a highly valued target.

Civil liberties and equal protection problems clearly emerge from this method of terrorism prevention. We must either deny overly broad ethnic categories of people access to targets and resources or we must develop detailed information about members of that group or aliens in general (also a form of discrimination) or about a far wider category of individuals (e.g., all U.S. citizens and residents).

There are real long-term costs to concentrating only on limited ethnic categories when the number of innocent people subjected to investigation or denial of access will vastly exceed the number of legitimate suspects. Every member of the class denied access or subjected to special investigation will be made to feel less than a full citizen of the United States or less than a welcome visitor, and that message eventually will be conveyed to all U.S. citizens.

Alternative Strategies

An alternative to either an ethnically-focused or alien-based monitoring strategy is to use high-powered computers to check all individuals in a large group equally before granting them access to targets or resources. This investigative technique requires three capabilities: (1) a reliable way to identify all individuals seeking access; (2) adequate and reliable intelligence information to identify dangerous people; and (3) an ability to match the two quickly, without great inconvenience. While our government currently lacks all three capacities for this form of prevention, the civil liberty costs will be

> *"[Those ethnic categories] denied access or subjected to special investigation will be made to feel less than a full citizen of the United States."*

great, when and if they are developed. *Every* individual will have to anticipate that: (1) increased amounts of personal information will likely be maintained on him or her by the government; (2) the government will monitor this information more frequently than in the past; (3) the possibility of separating oneself from one's own recorded personal history will become more difficult; and (4) the process of checking an individual's identity against recorded files may itself be designed to create and store new records of the individual's activities.

The use of such computerized systems will not await development of the missing capacities. Even without having complete or even substantial files to match with the identity of individuals seeking access to targets or resources, keeping records of those who are seeking such access may, in itself, be useful. Certain combinations of activities, when identified by intelligence agencies, can raise the suspicion necessary to monitor the individual and his immediate associates. For example, fermenters are used for making beer, but can also be used for making an anthrax weapon. An observation that someone who has no legitimate beer-brewing capacity has bought a fermenter may warrant beginning the first stages of an investigation. But collecting new information and combining it in newly revealing ways will reduce the privacy of many innocent individuals.

In creating new files for preventive purposes, we will be changing the traditional balance between law enforcement and internal security and the cultures associated with each. Almost every nation in the world has an internal security agency that is separate from its law enforcement agency, freed from many civil liberties constraints, and charged with providing the information the government needs (or the chief executive wants) for policy and political decisions and for prevention of dangerous situations. The United States has not taken that direction, instead giving only the FBI an internal intelligence function and narrowing that responsibility to focus almost entirely on counterespionage activities. That too will change.

Detaining Aliens

Detention. Finally, we can try to prevent a terrorist attack by detaining aliens who are in the United States illegally or are removable for cause, if they have had any association with those who have been connected with prior terrorist events. While noncitizens—resident aliens, visitors, and illegal entrants—are entitled to constitutional protections for criminal charges, they remain subject to arrest, detention, and questioning for any violation of the immigration laws that can lead to removal from the United States. When held for removal, noncitizens do not have a right to a free lawyer and their failure to speak may be used against them. Release pending departure can be denied. Detention of several months is thus an option generally available to the government. The President also has asserted the power to do this by executive order, even when there is no violation of immigration laws. In each case, the government would claim to be acting within its powers, although not for the immigration control purposes that justify granting detainment powers, and as it relates to the executive order, without congressional sanction.

The detention may be for purposes of interrogation pending trial or simply to incapacitate an individual for a sustained period of time. The decision of the attorney general, at least occasionally, to deny private access of detainees suspected of having terrorist ties even to their lawyers is a further effort to incapacitate the group. To the extent that the number of people detained is adequate to create a significant chance of interference with terrorist plans, these tactics will be effective.

> *"Granting exceptional authority to regulate, prohibit, search, and arrest presents dangers to the normal functioning of a democracy."*

Still, the strategy may be deeply flawed. It is worth exploring a less drastic alternative. By using "activity" categories, rather than nationality, we might increase arrests for crimes such as using or providing others with false identification papers or stealing credit cards or passports. A much higher percentage of those detained for such crimes might well prove to be dangerous and/or willing and able to provide information than the broader category of illegal aliens. And the technique would not discriminate on the basis of foreign origin or citizenship.

Using Emergency Powers

The key to consequence management is preparation: getting the committed physical and human resources into place, developing the necessary skills, advance training, and determining the proper scope of expanded legal authority required if and when a plausible threat or actual attack occurred. Planning for such eventualities requires envisioning a variety of terrorist scenarios, and the challenges that each presents for resources and governmental authority. The current capacities for consequence management—law enforcement, rescue and health resources and strong leadership to deal with psychological and political ramifications—are wholly inadequate for handling the aftermath of a major terrorist attack or the possible use of weapons of mass destruction.

> *"An irregular, military trial for actions taken within the borders of the United States shows an arrogant disdain for . . . the fairness of our courts."*

The critical question for civil liberties is what emergency legal authority should be made available to quarantine or relocate people, to command resources, to take or destroy property, and to search for extremely dangerous weapons. Granting exceptional authority to regulate, prohibit, search, and arrest presents dangers to the normal functioning of a democracy. Yet, such measures may be necessary in extraordinary circumstances. Any provision for such emergency powers must be designed to protect against misuse in ordinary times.

To provide for new legal powers to respond to major terrorist events, we must devise measures to ensure that such powers are available only in the most extraordinary instances, and that such determination is made by those who do not stand to benefit from the expanded powers. A court could approve a president's determination that a sufficient number of lives are at risk to justify invoking emergency powers, for example. Alternatively, the legislature could have the authority to override the president's invocation of emergency powers. In either case, it would be desirable to limit the powers to a relatively short time period.

The Use of Punishment

The United States has criminal statutes that apply to terrorists who attack Americans abroad. The Classified Information Protection Act allows the use of classified materials without unnecessarily compromising secrets. The witness protection program protects endangered witnesses, and a variety of mechanisms exist to protect jurors. Furthermore, we have, and have exercised on occasion, the capacity to bring terrorists back from across the world to stand trial in the United States. With this array of powers and authority, the United States has been able to prosecute the terrorists responsible for the first bombing of the World Trade Center, [on February 26, 1993], and the [twin] bombings of the U.S. embassies in Kenya and Tanzania, [on August 7, 1998], as well as Soviet spies, Mafia chieftains, and drug lords. I am not aware of any insuperable obstacles to trying dangerous terrorists in civil court, although obtaining strong evidence against those who sponsor terrorism can prove difficult.

On November 13, [2001], President [George W.] Bush signed an executive order allowing him to try non-U.S. citizens in military courts with penalties up to death for activities that the president determines to be involved in international terrorism or harboring international terrorists. The normal rules of evidence in civil cases will not apply; the trial can be closed; the members of a military panel need only decide by two-thirds; and there is no civilian judicial review of the decision (instead of review only by the president or the secretary of defense).

Without any showing of necessity, this assertion of power to punish even resident aliens after an irregular, military trial for actions taken within the borders of the United States shows an arrogant disdain for American pride in, and foreign admiration of, the fairness of our courts.

Our efforts to prevent future terrorist attacks, to deal with the consequences of massive attacks, and to punish terrorists are certain to result in some loss of civil liberties. But we should be careful not to trample democratic traditions unnecessarily. Exercising this care requires seeing where the greatest dangers lie: in the exercise of existing discretionary powers by those in the executive branch, rather than in the recently adopted statutory changes.

The Total Information Awareness System Violates Privacy Rights

by John Allen Paulos

About the author: *John Allen Paulos, a professor of mathematics at Temple University in Philadelphia, Pennsylvania, and adjunct professor of journalism at Columbia University in New York, is author of* Innumeracy, *a book that explains how numbers can lead to misinformed government policies, confused personal decisions, and susceptibility to pseudoscience.*

Let's start with a basic question: What is the purpose of the battle against terrorism? One answer, perhaps reflecting how most Americans see things, is that we want to feel safe. As philosopher Thomas Hobbes knew, what people want most from the state is protection, not freedom. To this end, and since terrorists appear relatively invulnerable to the usual deterrents, it follows that we would ideally intercept them before they carry out their attacks.

This is part of what is fueling policies like the incarcerations [of suspected members of Al Qaeda terrorists] at Guantanamo, the massive sweeps by the Immigration and Naturalization Service, the registration programs we've seen since [the terrorist attacks of] September 11, 2001, and more ominously, the Pentagon's proposed techno-surveillance system, Total Information Awareness (TIA). Headed by retired Vice Admiral John M. Poindexter of Iran-Contra notoriety, TIA will cost, by some estimates, upward of $200 million over three years. Initial funding of $10 million will help set up a system to "detect, classify, ID, track [and] preempt" future terrorists—pre-perpetrators, if you will—whom Poindexter hopes to spot before they do harm.

Using supercomputers, sophisticated software and data-mining techniques common in marketing, the TIA will maintain records on Americans' credit card purchases, plane flights, e-mails, prescriptions, book purchases, housing, legal proceedings, driver's licenses, rental permits and more, all in the hope of detecting suspicious patterns of activity—buying certain chemicals, say, or renting crop-dusting planes.

Upon detecting these supposedly telltale patterns, law enforcement would hope to stop pre-perpetrators before they commit crimes. It's a worthy goal, but in pursuing it the government will collect, integrate and evaluate extensive personal data on all of us, greatly compromising our privacy and perhaps even our political liberty. Is it worth the cost to society?

Doing the Math

Let's consider a mathematical approach to that question, one that derives from probability theory and the obvious fact that the vast majority of people of every ethnicity are not terrorists.

For the sake of argument, let's assume that eventually some system of information gathering and interpretation becomes so uncannily accurate that when it examines a future terrorist (someone with terrorist intentions), 99% of the time it will correctly identify him as a pre-perpetrator. Furthermore, when this system examines somebody who is harmless, 99% of the time the system will correctly identify him as harmless. In short, it makes a mistake only once every 100 times.

Now let's say that law enforcement apprehends a person using this technology. Given these assumptions, one might guess that the person would almost certainly be a terrorist. Right? Well, no. Even with the system's amazing data-mining powers, there would be only a tiny chance that the apprehended person would have gone on to commit a terrorist act if he had not been caught.

"The government will collect, integrate and evaluate extensive personal data on all of us, greatly compromising our privacy."

To see why this is so and to make the calculations easy, let's postulate a population of 300 million people of whom 1,000 are future terrorists. The system will correctly identify, we're assuming, 99% of these 1,000 people as future terrorists. Thus, since 99% of 1,000 is 990, the system will apprehend 990 future terrorists. Great.

But wait. There are, by assumption, 299,999,000 nonterrorists in our population, and the system will be right about 99% of them as well. Another way of saying this is that it will be wrong about 1% of these people. Since 1% of 299,999,000 equals 2,999,990, the system will swoop down on these 2,999,990 innocent people as well as on the 990 guilty ones, apprehending them all.

That is, the system will arrest almost 3 million innocent people, about 3,000 times the number of guilty ones. And that occurs, remember, only because we're assuming the system has these amazing powers of discernment. If its powers are anything like our present miserable predictive capacities, an even greater percentage of those arrested will be innocent.

Of course, this is an imagined scenario, and the numbers, percentages and assumptions are open to serious question. Nevertheless, the fact remains that since almost all people are innocent, the overwhelming majority of the people rounded up using any set of reasonable criteria will be innocent. And even though the system proposes only increased scrutiny rather than arrest of suspected future terrorists, such scrutiny might very well lead over time to a voluminously detailed government dossier on each of us. At the same time, since scrutiny without interdiction is unlikely to stop future terrorists from carrying out an attack, the system is likely to lead to little, if any, increase in security.

We want to feel safe as we go about our daily lives, but I submit that the proposed Total Information Awareness program is not conducive to a feeling of safety, much less to a feeling of freedom. Let's fight terrorism without ditching our commitment to privacy rights.

Secret Review Courts Foster Violations of Civil Liberties

by Charles Levendosky

About the author: *Charles Levendosky writes on constitutional issues and is the creator and editor of the* Casper [Wyoming] Star-Tribune*'s First Amendment website (FACT).*

On November 18, [2002], the U.S. Foreign Intelligence Surveillance Court of Review ruled the USA PATRIOT Act[1] grants the U.S. Department of Justice broader authority to subject American citizens to secret surveillance and searches. The secret court had to resort to word games in order to reach its conclusion.

The Purpose of the Secret Court

In 1978, Congress passed the Foreign Intelligence Surveillance Act (FISA), which created a secret federal court to hear DOJ [Department of Justice] applications and to grant orders approving electronic surveillance "for the purpose of obtaining foreign intelligence information." That was to have been its sole purpose. Through an executive order by President [Bill] Clinton in 1995, the court's authority was expanded to include physical searches.

The original FISA court had seven federal judges, appointed by the Chief Justice of the U.S. Supreme Court. . . . President [George W.] Bush expanded the court to include 11 members of the federal judiciary. Each year the FISA court approves approximately 1,000 orders for surveillance and searches.

If a DOJ application for a search and surveillance order is turned down, the U.S. Attorney General can appeal to the FISA court of review. The November

---

1. The act, also known as Uniting and Strengthening America by Providing Appropriate Tools Required to Intercept and Obstruct Terrorism Act, was signed into law on October 26, 2001. The act gives domestic law enforcement and international intelligence agencies broad powers to prevent and prosecute acts of terrorism.

18 ruling came as the result of the first appeal the review court has heard since FISA was enacted.

In late August [2002], the lower FISA court denied U.S. Attorney General John Ashcroft's request to use FISA surveillance orders for conducting criminal investigations. Ashcroft claims that the USA PATRIOT Act grants the wider authority for FISA searches and surveillances. The FISA court told Ashcroft he was wrong.

The FISA Act limits the special court's authority. It only allows secret searches and surveillance orders for the "primary purpose" of investigating foreign intelligence activities. However, the PATRIOT Act altered the wording regarding a search's purpose. Now, a FISA court order can be granted if the investigation of foreign intelligence activities is the "significant purpose" of the search

> *"It should be clear to any objective observer that a warrant issued by a secret court is immediately suspect."*

and surveillance. Ashcroft contends that means criminal activity can be the subject of a FISA search. Unfortunately, the FISA review court agrees with Ashcroft. It had to do some fancy dancing to arrive at its conclusion.

The Justice Department Argument

Hearings before the FISA review court are not adversarial as in most appeals courts. Only one side is presented. No one argued for the lower FISA court's position. Indeed, the DOJ was allowed to present the review court with an argument it had not even used at the lower FISA court.

The Justice Department argued the FISA court does not have the authority to question the government's intention to use search and surveillance orders only for the gathering of foreign intelligence information. The review court bought that argument, although the statutory language that creates the FISA court contradicts it.

In its ruling, the review court said by questioning the government's intention and by forcing the department to set up communication "fire walls" so prior evidence of criminal activity cannot be used to request a FISA order, the FISA court was intruding upon the executive branch's right to run its department without court interference.

This is patently nonsense. If a federal agency is breaking the law, a federal court has the duty to direct the agency to act in accordance with the law and if need be, to tell it how to do so.

The American Civil Liberties Union, Center for Democracy and Technology, Center for National Security Studies, Electronic Privacy Information Center and the Electronic Frontier Foundation filed a friend of the court brief in support of the lower FISA court's ruling, as did the National Association of Criminal Defense Lawyers.

A Questionable Ruling

Both friend of the court briefs questioned whether the broader application of FISA search and surveillance orders is consistent with the Fourth Amendment. It is here the review court reveals the weaknesses of its rationale.

The Fourth Amendment requires that a warrant be issued by a neutral, disinterested judge.

The FISA review court claims that "there is no dispute that a FISA judge satisfies the Fourth Amendment requirement of a "neutral and detached magistrate." Not so. It should be clear to any objective observer that a warrant issued by a secret court is immediately suspect—especially since the application for the order and the order itself are kept secret. The claim of neutrality is suspect when all but one of the tens of thousands of government applications for FISA court orders have been granted.

The review court admits that a FISA order does not require the same level of "probable cause" as required by the Fourth Amendment. An order can be issued if the activities "may involve" a violation of criminal statutes. The review court justifies the lower standard because these activities involve "domestic threats to national security."

And the review court admits, as it must, that FISA orders do not meet the Fourth Amendment requirement that warrants must particularly describe the things to be seized and places to be searched. Surveillance devices are left on continuously without oversight so people not named in the orders can be recorded for long periods of time.

Finally, the review court concludes, "we think the procedures and government showings required under FISA, if they do not meet the minimum Fourth Amendment warrant standards, certainly come close."

"Close" is not an adequate standard for the preservation of Fourth Amendment rights. The FISA court can approve clandestine break-ins of homes, monitoring a citizen's use of the Internet and the use of roving warrants to tap numerous telephones a person might use.

What can we expect of a secret review court, except more authority for secret courts?

Expanding FBI Intelligence-Gathering Powers Will Violate Civil Liberties

by Nat Hentoff

About the author: *Nat Hentoff often writes on civil liberties issues in his weekly* Village Voice *column. His work also appears in the* Wall Street Journal, *the* New York Times, *the* New Republic, Commonweal, *the* Atlantic *and the* New Yorker.

As usual, television—broadcast and cable—got it wrong. The thrust of what they call reporting on the reorganization of the FBI focused on the 900 or so new agents, the primacy of intelligence gathering over law enforcement, and the presence of CIA supervisors within the bosom of the FBI. (It used to be illegal for the CIA to spy on Americans within our borders.)

A Secret War Against Americans

But the poisonous core of this reorganization is its return to the time of J. Edgar Hoover and COINTELPRO, the counter-intelligence operation—pervasively active from 1956 to 1971—that so disgraced the Bureau that it was forced to adopt new guidelines to prevent such wholesale subversion of the Bill of Rights ever again.

Under COINTELPRO, the FBI monitored, infiltrated, manipulated, and secretly fomented divisions within civil rights, anti-war, black, and other entirely lawful organizations who were using the First Amendment to disagree with government policies.

These uninhibited FBI abuses of the Bill of Rights were exposed by some journalists, but most effectively by the Senate Select Committee to Study Governmental Operations With Respect to Intelligence Activities. Its chairman, Frank Church of Idaho, was a true believer in the constitutional guarantees of individual liberties against the government—which is why we had a Revolution.

In 1975, Church told the nation, and J. Edgar Hoover, that COINTELPRO had been "a sophisticated vigilante operation aimed squarely at preventing the exercise of First Amendment rights of speech and association." And Church pledged: "The American people need to be reassured that never again will an agency of the government be permitted to conduct a secret war against those citizens it considers a threat to the established order."

> *"[FBI] eavesdroppers do not need any evidence, not even a previous complaint, that anything illegal is going on, or is being contemplated."*

Frank Church, however, could not have foreseen George W. Bush, [attorney general] John Ashcroft, FBI director Robert Mueller, and the cowardly leadership, Republican and Democratic, of Congress. (Notable exceptions are John Conyers of Michigan, and Russell Feingold and James Sensenbrenner, both of Wisconsin.)

The guidelines for FBI investigations imposed after COINTELPRO ordered that agents could not troll for information in churches, libraries, or political meetings of Americans without some reasonable leads that someone, somehow, was doing or planning something illegal.

Throwing Away Protective Guidelines

Without even a gesture of consultation with Congress, Ashcroft unilaterally has thrown away those guidelines.

From now on, covert FBI agents can mingle with unsuspecting Americans at churches, mosques, synagogues, meetings of environmentalists, the ACLU [American Civil Liberties Union], the Gun Owners of America, and Reverend Al Sharpton's presidential campaign headquarters. (He has been resoundingly critical of the cutting back of the Bill of Rights.) These eavesdroppers do not need any evidence, not even a previous complaint, that anything illegal is going on, or is being contemplated.

Laura Murphy, the director of the ACLU's Washington office, puts the danger to us all plainly: "The FBI is now telling the American people. 'You no longer have to do anything unlawful in order to get that knock on the door.'"

During COINTELPRO, I got that knock on the door because I, among other journalists, had been publishing COINTELPRO reports that had been stolen from an FBI office. You might keep a pocket edition of the Constitution handy to present to the FBI agents—like a cross in front of Dracula.

The attorney general is repeatedly reassuring the American people that there's nothing to worry about. FBI agents, he says, can now go into any public place "under the same terms and conditions of any member of the public."

Really? While the rest of us do not expect privacy in a public place, we also do not expect to be spied upon and put into an FBI dossier because the organizers of the meeting are critical of the government, even of Ashcroft. We do not expect the casually dressed person next to us to be a secret agent of Ashcroft.

Former U.S. Attorney Zachary Carter, best known for his prosecution of the Abner Louima[1] case, said in the May 31, 2002, *New York Times* that Ashcroft's discarding of the post-COINTELPRO guidelines means, that now "law enforcement authorities could conduct investigations that [have] a chilling effect on entirely appropriate lawful expressions of political beliefs, the free exercise of religion, and the freedom of assembly."

So where are the cries of outrage from Democratic leaders Tom Daschle and Dick Gephardt? How do you tell them apart from the Republicans on civil liberties?

Back in 1975, Frank Church issued a warning that is far more pertinent now than it was then. He was speaking of how the government's intelligence capabilities—aimed at "potential" enemies, as well as disloyal Americans—could "at any time" be "turned around on the American people, and no American would have any privacy left—such is the capacity to monitor everything, telephone conversations, telegrams, it doesn't matter. There would be no place to hide. . . .

"There would be no way to fight back," Church continued, "because the most careful effort to combine together in resistance to the government, no matter how privately it was done, is within the reach of the government to know."

Frank Church could not foresee the extraordinary expansion of electronic surveillance technology, the government's further invasion of the Internet under the new Ashcroft-Mueller guidelines, nor the Magic Lantern [an FBI-developed computer program] that can record every keystroke you make on your computer. But Church's pessimism notwithstanding, there is—and surely will be—resistance. And I'd appreciate hearing from resisters who are working to restore the Bill of Rights.

---

1. Louima, a Haitian immigrant, was tortured by New York City police officers in 1997. Only Justin Volpe was convicted. The other three officers, Charles Schwarz, Thomas Wiese, and Thomas Bruder, were convicted of obstruction, though these convictions were set aside on February 28, 2002.

Intelligence Gathering to Prevent Economic Espionage Violates Civil Liberties

by Andrew Grosso

About the author: *Andrew Grosso is an attorney in Washington, D.C., and serves as chair of the Association for Computing Machinery's Committee on Law and Computer Technology.*

In order to protect homegrown secrets from foreign competitors, the U.S. Congress concocted the EEA, a cause of broad concern on the domestic front.

In 1996 the U.S. Congress passed the Economic Espionage Act (EEA). Viewed simply, the EEA criminalizes the theft of confidential business information. However, when dealing with information, few things involving criminalization are simple, and the EEA is not among those few.

The impetus for the EEA was the end of the Cold War. Suddenly, the U.S. found that the greatest threat to its well-being had changed from military opposition to economic competition. Considering itself to be a world leader in industrial innovation, the U.S. decided to ensure homegrown secrets of its native corporations would not be made available through theft and espionage to foreign competitors.

Significantly, the EEA did not limit its proscriptions to merely international espionage, but included prohibitions against domestic theft and use of confidential information in very broad terms. It is these broad prohibitions, when applied to the concept of "information," that make the EEA a dangerous legal companion for any worker, independent contractor, or employer involved in the information industry.

The EEA focuses on "trade secrets," a term with a statutory definition so expansive as to encompass anything a company may want to keep confidential, for any business motive whatsoever. The EEA reads:

> [A]ll forms and types of financial, business, scientific, technical, economic, or engineering information, including patterns, plans, compilations, programs, devices, formulas, designs, prototypes, methods, techniques, processes, procedures, programs or codes, whether tangible or intangible, and whether or how stored, compiled, or memorialized physically, electronically, graphically, photographically, or in writing. . . .

The EEA's scope is clearly not limited to intellectual property as that term is usually understood. If an employee has access to anything an employer deems confidential, then the employee is obligated to maintain the secrecy of that information, no matter how mundane or nonscientific the information may be. This is in sharp contrast to most state trade secret laws which generally highlight scientific or technical information, and on federal laws, which focus on copyrighted and patented works, or, implicitly, on state-defined trade secrets.

A Broad Definition of Espionage

The EEA also takes an expansive view of the meaning of theft or espionage. There is no requirement that an individual copy or otherwise duplicate the protected information as the manner or means of providing that information to a third party. Mere disclosure of that information, through any means whatsoever, for the "economic benefit of anyone other than the owner," is prohibited. The statute can be violated merely by employees changing jobs and using information learned in a prior position for the benefit of their new employer. This point was explicitly recognized by Congress in the legislative history of the EEA:

> The statute is not intended to be used to prosecute employees who change employers or start their own companies using general knowledge and skills developed while employed. It is the intent of Congress, however, to make criminal the acts of employees who leave their employment and use their knowledge about specific products for processing these in order to duplicate them or develop similar good for themselves or a new employer in order to compete with their prior employer.

Similarly, a company can find itself in violation of the EEA by hiring employees away from competitors, and then putting them to work on projects similar to those previously handled for those competitors.

In the past, civil suits have been brought against companies, based upon state law, for conversion of trade secrets accomplished through the hiring of a competitor's employee. Such civil prosecutions have been approved by some courts. Given this track record, as well as the express congressional intent that the EEA be used by the Department of Justice to criminally punish this type of activity, both employers and employees are well advised to think carefully about the role of a new employee when that person has valuable expertise learned at a previous job with a competitor employer. Independent contractors, similarly, must be careful about using information learned through working on one client's matter for the benefit of a later client.

Reverse engineering also falls under the EEA. This is clear from the charging language:

> Whoever, with intent to convert a trade secret, that is related to or included in a product . . . , to the economic benefit of anyone other than the owner thereof, and intending or knowing that the offense will injure any owner of that trade secret, knowingly . . . (2) without authorization copies, duplicates, sketches, draws, photographs, downloads, uploads, alters, destroys, photocopies, replicates, transmits, delivers, sends, mails, communicates, or conveys such information . . . shall [be punished as provided in the EEA].

Put simply, analyzing a competitor's product in order to replicate the code or process by which it functions, with the intent of manufacturing a similar or complementary product that might impede the economic opportunities of said competitor, falls under the prohibitions of the EEA.

The Threat to Civil Liberties

Civil liberties continue to collide with the new laws of the information age. The EEA is no exception.

First, the EEA permits federal law enforcement authorities to use wiretaps in order to investigate violations of the EEA. Wiretaps are one of the most intrusive of all investigative techniques, second only to the outright arrest of a suspect or a search and seizure. Typically, they are reserved for violent or organized crime investigations. Authorization to use wiretaps in what is essentially a crime against property represents another step toward advancing interests of commerce over the integrity of the individual in the information age.

Second, the EEA limits what a person can and cannot disclose regarding knowledge obtained through legitimate means, for example, through prior employment. This prohibition is profoundly different than other intellectual property statutes, such as patent and copyright laws, which generally proscribe what can be done with knowledge rather than prohibiting mere disclosure. The difference is significant: manufacturing a commercial product via patent infringement is clearly a crime against property, whereas disclosing information, even

> *"Broad prohibitions . . . make the [Economic Espionage Act] a dangerous legal companion for any worker, independent contractor, or employer in the information industry."*

confidential information, includes an element of speech. For this reason, the EEA runs perilously close to infringing the First Amendment right of free speech. Aside from the chilling effect the EEA has on constitutionally protected conduct, this fact may provide grounds for a successful defense in some future prosecution, especially where the government has failed to adequately investigate or prove an overt act on the part of the defendant to use or further the use of the purloined knowledge for the economic benefit of a third party (or for the defendant).

Third, the EEA requires, in any prosecution or other proceeding, that a court "enter such order and take such other action as may be necessary and appropriate to preserve the confidentiality of trade secrets . . ." not inconsistent with other statutory requirements. This provision is in direct conflict with traditional and deeply rooted notions of due process in our criminal justice system: defendants have a right to know all the evidence being used against them, to challenge that evidence, and to challenge such evidence in an open trial before the public. This provision is meant to prevent confidential information from being made public when the government brings a criminal prosecution against someone. However, in a criminal trial, this provision would tend to prevent a defendant from learning what the significant aspect of the information he or she is accused of disclosing; prevent the defendant from disclosing that information to third parties, including expert witnesses and competitors, in order to evaluate and challenge that aspect; and prevent the defendant from attacking the information and its significance in open court. In summary, it is difficult to see what force and effect any court can give to this provision if a defendant is to be given a fair trial. Nonetheless, Congress is serious in this regard—it also authorized prosecutors to take interlocutory appeals to federal appellate courts, that is, to stop a prosecution in mid-stream and appeal to a higher tribunal in those instances where trial judges have not, in the opinion of the prosecutors, adequately protected the confidentiality of the information which is the subject of the case.

> *"Authorization to use wiretaps . . . represents another step toward advancing interests of commerce over the integrity of the individual."*

The Threat to Victims

One should not labor under the impression that the EEA's pitfalls are all one-sided. Specifically, one should not overlook the difficulties that victims of trade secret theft will have using the EEA as a remedy.

To be considered a trade secret, the EEA requires more than just that the information be valuable. It also requires that (1) the owner take "reasonable measures" to maintain the secrecy of the information, and (2) the value of the information to the owner is somehow derived from the fact that it is secret.

The first of these requirements places an obligation on the information's owner. A company cannot treat its trade secrets in a cavalier manner and then expect the EEA to be applicable. More to the point, one cannot merely assume that one's employees and coworkers recognize as a matter of course that secrecy is important to a project.

Instead, a company must take affirmative and open steps to make clear to all concerned that the information is confidential; to impose procedures designed to protect against disclosure, accidental or otherwise; and to publicize the fact that disclosure of the pertinent information will incur penalties, such as loss of one's job. As a policy matter, these requirements may very well be difficult to implement in those technical environments where the free flow of information is taken as a matter of course, and where continued advances in state-of-the-art developments depend upon such flow.

Finally, invocation of the EEA may be equivalent to destroying a village in order to save it. Once the matter is brought to the attention of law enforcement authorities, a victim company loses substantially all control over the prosecution of the matter, and, ultimately, over whether the subject information will be made public in a trial or discovery proceeding. The Department of Justice makes the decision whether or not to press charges under federal criminal laws, and it may choose to do so even after a victim company subsequently recognizes it is not in its best interest for such a prosecution to go forward. The reasons why a company may reach this conclusion are numerous, and may include the risk of bad publicity, public disclosure of the trade secret, adverse effects on stock value due to the publicity or trade secret disclosure, and the reaching of a separate accommodation with the perpetrator. These concerns do not motivate a prosecutor, who may be more concerned with the deterrent effect to the industry at large resulting from a single prosecution than with any adverse effects a particular company may suffer from that prosecution. Moreover, once an indictment has been issued, a defendant has an opportunity to obtain and use publicly, in his or her defense, the very information the company wishes to preserve as secret. The results of an EEA prosecution, particularly one that proceeds completely to trial, will usually include the irrevocable and public disclosure of the very information whose value is founded in secrecy. For these reasons, companies will want to think twice about bringing theft of a trade secret to the attention of law enforcement authorities if there is any chance the damage due to a disclosure is limited, and if the overall confidentiality of the subject information, and therefore its value, can somehow still be maintained.

Criminal statutes are supposed to be clearly, intelligently, and narrowly drawn. The reason for this is the requirement that, under the constitution, no person may be deprived of life, liberty, or property without due process, that is, without fundamental fairness in an adversarial proceeding. What, then, can be more basic to such fairness than a clear, intelligent, and narrow drafting of the proscribed conduct that the state intends to punish?

The EEA fails to satisfy this standard. What is more puzzling than its many problems, however, is that the problems exist for both victims and accused. Given the EEA's breadth and application to the information industry, it would be wise for all professionals to develop some understanding of where the traps are for the unwary.

136

Granting Intelligence Agencies Increased Powers to Fight Terrorism Does Not Threaten Civil Liberties

by Viet D. Dinh

About the author: *Viet D. Dinh is assistant attorney general, U.S. Department of Justice. Before government service, Dinh was a professor and the deputy director of Asian Law and Policy Studies at the Georgetown University Law Center.*

The core meaning of . . . [the] concept [of ordered liberty] is profoundly relevant to our current war against terror. Some have suggested that the actions we have taken to prosecute that war are a threat to liberty; others defend those actions as vital to the preservation of our liberty. I seek today to mediate these opposing viewpoints by exploring the meaning of ordered liberty. This return to first principles may seem pedantic to this audience, well versed in law and jurisprudence. With your indulgence, I think it is important at this time of peril for us to take stock of certain basic questions: 1) what is it we are fighting for; 2) who is it we are fighting against; and 3) how are we to wage this fight?

The Concept of Ordered Liberty

When the nation is under attack, the natural answer to the first question, what are we fighting for, is: for the security of America and the safety of her people. That answer naturally pits security against other societal values and leads some to recite Benjamin Franklin's now-famous statement, "they that can give up essential liberty to obtain a little temporary safety deserve neither liberty nor safety."

That we are fighting for security and safety is a true enough answer, but I do not think it is a complete answer. In this sense I agree with Franklin and those who quote him that one should not trade liberty (let alone *essential* liberty) for

Viet D. Dinh, address before the District of Columbia Bar, Annual Judge Leventhal Lecture Series on Ordered Liberty, July 7, 2002. Copyright © 2002 by Viet D. Dinh. Reproduced by permission.

safety (let alone *a little temporary* safety). But the trade-off between security and liberty is a false choice. That is so because security should not be (and under our constitutional democracy, is not) an end in itself, but rather simply a means to the greater end of liberty.

However, my agreement with Franklin's statement does not settle the debate but only begins the conversation. For the essential question is, What do we mean by liberty? Here, I think [political philosopher] Edmund Burke puts it best: "The only liberty I mean is a liberty connected with order, that not only exists along with order and virtue, but which cannot exist at all without them." In other words, ordered liberty. Order and liberty, under this conception, are symbiotic; each is necessary to the stability and legitimacy that is essential for a government under law.

To illustrate this symbiotic relationship, consider liberty without order. Absent order, liberty is simply unbridled license: Men can do whatever they choose. It is easy enough to recognize that such a world, of liberty without order, is unstable, but I would argue that it is also illegitimate. A liberty of unbridled license is no liberty at all. As [philosopher Jean-Jacques] Rousseau recognized, "Liberty does not consist as much in acting according to one's own will as in not being subjected to the will of anyone else." In a world of unbridled license, the strong do what they will and the weak suffer what they must. One man's expression of his desires will deprive another man of his license. Liberty without order is therefore both unstable and illegitimate—illegitimacy resulting from the infringement, by force as necessary, on one man's freedom by another's desire.

Our founders recognized this danger of unbridled license. Fisher Ames declared in 1787: "Liberty we had, but we dreaded its abuse almost as much as its loss; and the wise, who deplored the one, clearly foresaw the other." True liberty only exists in an ordered society with rules and laws that govern the behavior of men.

Order Without Liberty

Just as liberty cannot exist without order, order without liberty is not only illegitimate but also unstable. The first of these propositions is widely accepted, so I will not dwell on it here. But it is important to recognize that where there is only order but not liberty, force must be exerted by men over men in an attempt to compel obedience and create a mirage of stability. Most people are familiar with Rousseau's dictum

> *"The trade-off between security and liberty is a false choice."*

that "Man was born free, yet everywhere he is in chains." But often neglected is the sentence that immediately follows in *On the Social Contract*: "He who believes himself the master of others is nonetheless a greater slave than they. . . . For in recovering its freedom by means of the same right used to steal it, either the people are justified in taking it back, or those who took it away were not justified in doing so."

Order without liberty is unstable precisely because it is illegitimate. In an apparent order maintained by brute strength, the ruler has no greater claim to the use of force than his subject, and the master and slave are in a constant state of war—one trying to maintain the mirage of stability created by his use of force, the other seeking to use force to recover his lost freedom.

Order and liberty, therefore, are not competing concepts that must be balanced against each other to maintain some sort of democratic equilibrium. Rather, they are complementary values that contribute symbiotically to the stability and legitimacy of a constitutional democracy. Order and liberty go together like love and marriage and horse and carriage; you can't have one without the other.

In *The Structure of Liberty*, Professor Randy Barnett distinguishes liberty structured by order from unbridled license by comparing it to a tall building, the Sears Tower. License permits thousands of people to congregate in the same space, but only with the order imposed by the structure of the building—its hallways and partitions, stairwells and elevators, signs and lights—would those thousands be endowed with liberty, each to pursue his own end without trampling on others or being trampled on. "Like a building, every society has a structure that, by constraining the actions of its members, permits them at the same time to act to accomplish the ends." To illustrate the essential necessity of that structure, Barnett posits this hypothetical: "Imagine being able to push a button and make the structure of the building instantly vanish. Thousands of persons would plunge to their deaths."

> *"A liberty of unbridled license is no liberty at all."*

Attacking the Foundation of Ordered Liberty

[Terrorist] Osama bin Laden pushed that button on September 11, [2001], and thousands of persons plunged to their deaths. Just as Barnett's Sears Tower was only a metaphor for the structure of ordered liberty, Al Qaeda's aim was not simply to destroy the World Trade Center. Its target was the very foundation of our ordered liberty.

Knowing what we now know about Al Qaeda, it is easy to see that its radical, extremist ideology is incompatible with, and an offense to, ordered liberty. Al Qaeda seeks to subjugate women; we work for their liberation. Al Qaeda seeks to deny choice; we celebrate the marketplace of ideas. Al Qaeda seeks to suppress speech, we welcome open discussion.

More fundamental, however, is the proposition that Al Qaeda, simply by adopting the way of terror, attacks the foundation of our ordered liberty. Terrorism, whomever its perpetrator and whatever his aim, poses a fundamental threat to the ordered liberty that is the essence of our constitutional democracy.

The terrorist seeks not simply to kill, but to terrorize. His strategy is not merely to increase the count of the dead, but to bring fear to those who survive. The terrorist is indiscriminate in his choice of victims and indifferent about the value of his targets. Part of an international conspiracy of evil, he operates across boundaries and recognizes no borders. He uses violence to disrupt order, kills to foment fear, and terrorizes to incapacitate normal human activity. Thus, by definition, the methods and objectives of terror attack the foundation of ordered liberty.

> *"Terrorism . . . poses a fundamental threat to the ordered liberty that is the essence of our constitutional democracy."*

In this sense, the terrorist is fundamentally different from the criminal offender normally encountered by our criminal justice system. By attacking the foundation of order in our society, the terrorist seeks to demolish the structure of liberty that governs our lives. By fomenting terror among the masses, the terrorist seeks to incapacitate the citizenry from exercising the liberty to pursue our individual ends. This is not criminality. It is a war-like attack on our polity.

Facing a New Enemy

In waging that war, the terrorist employs means that fundamentally differ from those used by the traditional enemies we have faced on the battlefield according to the established rules of war among nations. Those rules clearly distinguish uniformed combatants who do battle with each other from innocent civilians who are off-target—a distinction that is not only ignored but exploited by the terrorist to his advantage. In this war, the international terrorist against whom we fight differs even from guerilla warriors of past who mingle among civilians and, at times, target innocent civilians. The evil activities of the terrorist is not limited to some hamlet in Southeast Asia or remote village in Latin America. For the international terrorist, the world is his battleground, no country is immune from attack, and all innocent civilians are exposed to the threat of wanton violence and incapacitated by the fear of terror.

This, then, is the enemy we face. A criminal whose objective is not crime but fear. A mass murderer who kills only as a means to a larger end. A predator whose victims are all innocent civilians. A warrior who exploits the rules of war. A war criminal who recognizes no boundaries and who reaches all corners of the world.

The Prevention Paradigm

How, then, do we confront this enemy? The valiant efforts of our men and women on the battlefield in Afghanistan [to defeat the Taliban, Afghanistan's ruling regime which harbored al-Qaeda members] and the constant vigilance of our men and women in blue on the streets of America are the traditional responses—traditional and essential in this effort. But for the Department of Justice, we needed a fundamentally different approach to the way we approached the traditional task of law enforcement. Unlike traditional soldiers, terrorists wage war dressed not in green camouflage but in the colors of street clothing. Unlike traditional criminals, terrorists are willing to sacrifice their own lives in order to take the lives of innocents. We cannot afford to wait for terrorists to execute their plans; the death toll is too high; the consequences too great.

That is why since [the] September 11, [2001, terrorist attacks], the Department has refocused its investigative and prosecutorial resources toward one overriding and overarching objective: to prevent terrorist attacks before they happen and to disrupt terrorist activities before they threaten innocent lives. This massive effort is undertaken with one objective, to defend the foundations of our ordered liberty—to deliver freedom from fear by protecting freedom through law.

Taking Steps to Preserve Freedom

First, we have sought to create an airtight surveillance net of terrorist activity by updating the law to reflect new technologies. Law enforcement had been operating at a technologically competitive disadvantage with the terrorists. We have corrected that. Congress passed the USA Patriot Act to extend the capacity of law enforcement to monitor communications in the digital, as well as the analog world. The Attorney General revised the Department's investigative guidelines to enhance the FBI's ability to conduct on line searches on the same terms and conditions as the general public. With each of these steps, and for each of these tools, we were careful not to alter the substantive legal predicates that exist to preserve the privacy of law abiding citizens.

"The terrorist employs means that fundamentally differ from those used by the traditional enemies we have faced on the battlefield."

Second, we have enhanced the capacity of law enforcement to gather and analyze intelligence on terrorist activity. The USA Patriot Act authorized the sharing of intelligence information across government departments so that we can compile the mosaic of information required to prevent terrorism. And the recent revisions to the AG [Attorney General] guidelines prompts the FBI to adopt a proactive role in investigating terrorist activity. The revisions devolve authority to conduct terrorist investigations to the field offices, freeing up the hands of agents to gather the pieces of the investigative puzzle. And it centralized information for analysis, so that all the pieces of the puzzle can be fitted at a single table. We have created a real-world document that will actually govern the actions of investigators—empowering their discretion where appropriate and clearly specifying the limits of their authority where necessary. These revisions, therefore, will not only enhance terrorist investigations but also reaffirm the freedom of law-abiding citizens from unnecessary intrusion.

Finally, we have employed a deliberate strategy to remove from our streets those who would seek to do us harm. We utilize our prosecutorial discretion to the fullest extent in order to incapacitate suspected terrorists from fulfilling their plans. Robert F. Kennedy's Justice Department, it was said, would arrest a mobster for spitting on the sidewalk, and Eliot Ness brought down Al Capone for tax evasion. We have sought to apply this approach to the war on terror. Any infraction, however minor, will be prosecuted against suspected terrorists. However, each and every person detained arising from our investigation into 9/11 has been detained with an individualized predicate—a criminal charge, an immigration violation, or a judicially issued material witness warrant. We do not engage in Preventive Detention. In this respect, our detention policy differs significantly from those of other countries, which can subject individuals to preventive detention simply to prevent them from committing a crime. In fact, the European Convention on Human Rights allows states to subject a person to preventive detention "when it is reasonably considered necessary to prevent his committing an offence."

Preserving the Law

In short, in prosecuting the war of terror, we have taken every step at our discretion, used every tool at our disposal, and employed every authority under the law to prevent terrorism and defend our ordered liberty. We have done so with the constant reminder that it is liberty we are preserving and with scrupulous attention to the legal and constitutional safeguards of those liberties. The Attorney General's charge to the Department after 9/11 was simple: Think outside the box, but never outside of the Constitution.

On the walls of the Department of Justice are inscribed the following words: "Where law ends tyranny begins." John Locke wrote that "the end of law is not to abolish or restrain but to preserve and enlarge freedom.". . . [On June 6, 2002], the President of Harvard University conferred degrees on its law graduates, as he has done for the past half-century, by defining law as "the system of wise restraints that set men free." And when Attorney General Ashcroft welcomed me to the Department, he wrote, "It is a profound honor to work with you in defense of freedom."

The common thread that weaves these different voices and timeless phrases is law. Law as the guardian of order. Law as the protector of liberty. Law, in short, as the structure of ordered liberty that is under attack and to whose defense we are now called.

I close, therefore, with the words of Daniel Webster, spoken at a gathering of lawyers in 1847, when he raised his glass in a toast and said, "To the law. It has honored us; may we honor it."

The Total Information Awareness System Does Not Violate Privacy Rights

by Jeff Carley

About the author: *Jeff Carley is the chief technology officer for Engedi Technologies, Inc., a company that develops network security products.*

On September 11, 2001, the passengers of United Airlines Flight 93 rushed their hijackers, who caused the plane to crash into a field about 80 miles southeast of Pittsburgh. What enabled those passengers to take action to try to stop the hijackers, while on three other planes that morning the hijackers were able to strike high-profile targets and kill thousands of people on the ground? Information, in part, was that critical differentiating element. The passengers on Flight 93 had the right information at the right time to make a decision that probably saved hundreds of other American lives. They knew the hijackers were really terrorists who had to be stopped. The passengers were heroes. But I am sure there were brave men and women on the other flights who would have taken similar heroic action had they only known what was intended.

Information proved the critical element in enabling the passengers of Flight 93 to stop the terrorists confronting them. The passengers on the other flights lacked that critical information.

Making Sacrifices

We already have made sacrifices to protect ourselves as a result of the terrorist activities, and we likely will need to make more in the future. War is like that. One example is increased airport security. Those of us who travel by air try to be more tolerant of carry-on-baggage checks, longer lines at security checkpoints and random searches. And if you are flying into Ronald Reagan Washington National Airport, be careful not to drink too much coffee, because you will not be allowed to get out of your seat to go to the bathroom during the last half-hour of the flight. Our world has changed in big and little ways. It's not as convenient.

We already have sacrificed some of our privacy rights. War is like that. An appeals court recently ruled that the Justice Department has broad powers to use wiretaps under the USA PATRIOT Act. This will permit us to cast a wider net while looking for possible terrorist activity. Foreign nationals can be held without immediately being charged with a crime. With the passage of the Homeland Security bill, a number of agencies are being realigned, allowing them better to coordinate the information they have about us. These changes would be intolerable were it not for the current situation.

Using Information to Thwart Terrorists

Even so our nation is quite vulnerable to attack. As a freedom-loving people, we do not easily or lightly take the steps necessary to shut down all the possible avenues of attack from terrorists. Why is it necessary that we act now to analyze and use the information available to us? Because our enemy has chosen to hide among us. He pretends to be one of us while planning and preparing for the next attack. He chooses civilian targets of opportunity. He does not put on a uniform that says, "I am your enemy." This war is like that. To protect ourselves we must access and sift through all available information to uncover and thwart the enemies among us.

If we do not find better ways to use the information at hand to identify enemies in our midst, greater restrictions to our civil liberties could be triggered by the next terrorist act. To stop terrorists, the government needs as much information about them as possible. Lacking that information, or the effective use of available information, the government may be forced to place more restrictive and sweeping controls on the entire population.

The broader wiretap authority for the Justice Department is an example of the diminution of our privacy that allows the government to gather the information it needs. The inspections and restrictions involved in air travel are examples of the government controlling the entire population to control the terrorists. These blanketing restrictions could spread further into our lives if we fail to make appropriate and timely use of the information available.

Consider the situation in Israel, which is fielding a largely conventional military force against soldiers who have chosen to blend into a civilian population. Israel has restricted the liberty of its Jewish citizens and even more greatly restricted the liberties of the Palestinian population in which a jihadist enemy has hidden. Yet horrible acts of terrorism still occur. Whatever your opinion of the Israeli-Palestinian conflict, it does not change the fact that one mode of warfare from

> *"To stop terrorists, the government needs as much information about them as possible."*

the conflict has arrived in our land—terrorism—along with those who would commit these acts. We must be most effective in rooting out these terrorists.

The United States is an information-based society. We need to capitalize on our advantages. Our sophisticated computer technology can assimilate the data gathered by various interconnected computer networks and identify the characteristics of terrorist activity, as well as the threats they pose. Researchers at the Department of Defense have begun to develop the Total Information Awareness (TIA) system. This system would sift through massive amounts of data, correlating information from a wide variety of existing sources, comparing the information to established patterns consistent with terrorist activity and flagging those situations most in need of attention.

This system also would address one of the biggest complaints in the aftermath of September 11. Many people think various agencies had sufficient information to know that something was about to happen before September 11 and should have acted to prevent the attacks. However, correlating this information and deriving useful knowledge is not an easy task. Add in the past explicit discouragement of information-sharing in some situations, often due to privacy concerns, and it proved quite difficult to put all the pieces together. Putting the pieces together quickly and correctly involves the analysis of incredible volumes of information. It

"The overall effect of [Total Information Awareness] would be to increase the privacy of the average citizen."

is challenging to identify which pieces of information are critical to knowing when to sound the alarm. Computers are far more adept at filtering and looking for patterns than are humans. The flow of information is too great and complex for humans alone.

A System of Safeguards

Could a system such as TIA pose its own threat to our privacy? Access would be granted to massive amounts of raw data on just about every type of transaction taking place in our society. That in itself could be a danger if there are no safeguards. Fortunately such safeguards are an integral part of the proposed system. Research projects are underway to determine the best methods to protect information about innocent civilians while searching for signs of terrorist activities. One approach is to develop ways to safeguard the identity associated with specific data and only reveal that information, to authorized personnel, when a sought pattern is detected. Another approach is to anonymize data whenever possible. When searching for early signs of a biological attack, only geographic and demographic information about the recipient of a prescription is needed, not their identity.

The overall effect of TIA would be to increase the privacy of the average citizen by more clearly highlighting and then targeting the terrorists. An effective detection system would allow law enforcement better to focus on activity that matches the established patterns of interest. This would afford greater protection to privacy of activity that does not match patterns.

TIA could be the key to our long-term victory over terrorism. As is often the case with such tools, it can be a double-edged sword. Today, the purpose of developing such a system is to identify activity associated with terrorism. Tomorrow, it could be used for ferreting out activity associated with organized crime. Would patterns associated with pedophilia or child

> *"[Total Information Awareness] will offer greater security while at the same time protecting privacy rights of innocent people."*

pornography also be an acceptable use of TIA? Perhaps so, but that is another matter for another time.

Our best protection from the abuse of a system such as TIA is not prohibiting the research on how to do it, but rather ensuring its acceptable use and applying strong oversight to safeguard access to the system. TIA will offer greater security while at the same time protecting privacy rights of innocent people.

A New Weapon in a New War

Our nation is in a new kind of war. We need an innovative tool such as TIA for our defense. This war is being fought on our soil, and we are fighting for our existence. There is no truce or quarter being offered in this conflict. We cannot afford to decide that it is costing too much or making us too uncomfortable, and shy away from the task at hand. We must win this war. Long after we have defeated the current enemy, we will need to stay vigilant and armed to ensure new enemies do not strike.

Too often, we have expected our armed services and law-enforcement officers to protect us and our national interests around the world while not providing them with all they need to best accomplish their missions. Today, one critical need is the effective analysis and use of information. They need the right information at the right time to make the right decisions to defend our nation. With the right information, they can step heroically up to whatever is required.

America is at war, and to survive we must adapt to this new style of warfare. We need to hasten the development and implementation of new tools, such as TIA, that capitalize on our strengths and provide an advantage. We need TIA for our current conflict, and we will need it in the future. Yes, safeguards need to be built to ensure it is not abused, but without TIA our reactions to the ongoing threat of terrorism may leave us no choice but to accept sweeping restrictions that erode our civil liberties and degrade the quality of our lives far more. TIA is a powerful weapon to create. We need new and powerful weapons to win. War is like that.

Secret Review Courts Do Not Foster Violations of Civil Liberties

by Stuart Taylor Jr.

About the author: *Stuart Taylor Jr. is a senior writer and columnist on legal affairs for the* National Journal, *a weekly magazine covering politics and government, and a contributing editor at* Newsweek.

> One [FBI] agent, frustrated at encountering the "wall" [separating intelligence officials from criminal investigators], wrote to headquarters [on Aug. 29, 2001]: "Someday someone will die and—wall or not—the public will not understand why we were not more effective and throwing every resource we had at certain 'problems.' The biggest threat to us now, [terrorist] UBL [Osama bin Laden], is getting the most 'protection.'"
>
> —Opinion of Foreign Intelligence Surveillance
> Court of Review, November 18, 2002

Complexity can confound clear thinking and facilitate false alarms. Such has been the case with the claims that the above-quoted ruling by the special three-judge review court eviscerates our liberty and privacy rights. The powerfully reasoned decision held that the government may use the Foreign Intelligence Surveillance Act [FISA] to wiretap and search suspected agents of foreign terrorist groups and governments even if its primary goal is criminal prosecution, as distinguished from pure intelligence-gathering. It also dismantled the legal "wall" that has impeded intelligence officials from working with criminal investigators—a wall that may have made it easier for the September 11, [2001], hijackers to do their evil work.

But the complexity of issues involving FISA has enabled critics to cry wolf in a most misleading fashion, while some of the same folks who have deplored the failure of intelligence and law enforcement officials to work together now lament a ruling that will help them do just that.

The "misguided" review court, yelped *The New York Times*, "handed the government broad new authority . . . to wiretap phone calls, intercept mail, and spy on Internet use of ordinary Americans." This ruling, asserted the American Civil Liberties Union, "will affect every American's privacy rights" and "suspend the ordinary requirements of the Fourth Amendment."

Well. It *was* a big win for Attorney General John D. Ashcroft, whose habit of pushing his powers to dubious extremes does scare many of us. But the reports of liberty's death are greatly exaggerated. Let's explore 1) the previously obscure realm of FISA, which has become a critical tool in our government's efforts to stop terrorists before they kill us; 2) how the now-defunct "wall" has hindered those efforts; and 3) the modest impact of this decision on the more than 280 million Americans who are not foreign agents.

FISA and the Special Courts

FISA was enacted in 1978, initially for electronic surveillance, and later amended to cover physical searches, too. It required presidents—who had previously claimed unilateral power to wiretap or search suspected foreign agents—to obtain judicial warrants. At the same time, it relaxed the usual Fourth Amendment rule requiring "probable cause" to suspect criminal activities before approving wiretaps or searches, in light of the difficulty of producing such evidence in investigations of suspected foreign agents, who are trained to avoid suspicious activities. FISA requires somewhat less evidence—probable cause to suspect that the target is a foreign agent—while authorizing more-intrusive surveillance, for longer periods, under greater secrecy.

The statute created two special federal courts that operate in extraordinary (and to some extent unwarranted) secrecy. The so-called FISA court, recently expanded from seven to 11 judges, considers applications for warrants. The review court—federal appellate Judges Laurence H. Silberman of Washington, Edward Leavy of Portland, Oregon, and Ralph B. Guy Jr. of Ann Arbor, Michigan, all Reagan appointees—hears any government appeals from the FISA court. Both are staffed by federal judges from around the country designated by Chief Justice William H. Rehnquist to work part-time on FISA matters. The review court's November 18, [2002], decision was its first ever: The FISA court has approved almost all of the Justice Department's more than 14,000 warrant applications since 1978. This has led critics to dismiss the FISA court as a meaningless

> *"[The Foreign Intelligence Surveillance Act] dismantled the legal 'wall' that has impeded intelligence officials from working with criminal investigators."*

rubber stamp. Recent revelations suggest otherwise, and the government's batting average may instead reflect a policy of seeking informal guidance first and filing formal applications only when approval seems assured.

The FISA court showed its teeth [in August 2002] . . . in its much-publicized 7-0 decision that rejected Ashcroft's proposal to tear down the "wall," which is shorthand for a tangle of FISA court rules designed to prevent the government from seeking FISA warrants primarily for use in criminal prosecutions. The USA-PATRIOT Act[1] explicitly discarded some of these rules. But the FISA court adhered to others that barred prosecutors from advising intelligence officials on FISA matters and required that official "chaperones" attend meetings to ensure compliance. The review court reversed this decision. It also rejected the implication in the FISA court's opinion—which was internally inconsistent and thus incoherent on this point—that the government may not use FISA when its primary purpose is to prosecute terrorist conspiracies, espionage, or similar crimes.

How the "Wall" Protected Terrorists

The FISA court was right to bar the use of FISA to seek evidence for ordinary prosecution. (It's undisputed that any evidence of crime that turns up as an incidental result of a FISA search or wiretap can be so used.) But its notion that FISA could not be used to facilitate even prosecutions for terrorist conspiracies or espionage turned FISA's stated goal of "protect[ing] against" such dangers on its head. In the review court's words, "Arresting and prosecuting terrorist agents . . . or spies

"The reports of liberty's death are greatly exaggerated."

may well be the best technique to prevent . . . their terrorist or espionage activity." The "wall" not only made investigators wary of talking to one another. It also spurred unnatural contortions to eschew the natural impulse to use FISA to protect against terrorists or spies *by locking them up*.

"Indeed," the review court noted, "it was suggested that the FISA court requirements . . . may well have contributed, whether correctly understood or not, to the FBI missing opportunities to anticipate the September 11, 2001, attacks. . . . An FBI agent recently testified [in congressional hearings] that efforts to conduct a criminal investigation of two of the alleged hijackers were blocked by senior FBI officials—understandably concerned about prior FISA court criticism [for undisclosed or concealed breaches in the 'wall']—who interpreted that court's decisions as precluding a criminal investigator's role." Citing the FBI agent's bitter complaint that "someday someone will die"—because of the refusal of FBI headquarters to launch an aggressive search for Khalid Almihdhar, whom the CIA had identified as a bin Laden follower—the review court noted that the official response had been that "those were the rules, and [FBI

1. The act, also known as Uniting and Strengthening America by Providing Appropriate Tools Required to Intercept and Obstruct Terrorism Act, was signed into law on October 26, 2001. The act gives domestic law enforcement and international intelligence agencies broad powers to prevent and prosecute acts of terrorism.

headquarters] does not make them up." Thirteen days later, Almihdhar helped crash an airliner into the Pentagon.

Why did the FISA court create such strange rules? They are rooted in decisions by other federal courts that the Fourth Amendment bars seeking a FISA warrant primarily for the purpose of prosecution. Those decisions in turn cite Supreme Court precedents arguably establishing a general rule that any searches and wiretaps aimed primarily at prosecution must be authorized in advance by warrants based—unlike some FISA warrants—on "probable cause" to suspect criminal activity. But that rule was not designed to deal with the terrorists who now threaten us with mass murders dwarfing the harm done by ordinary criminals. And almost all rules have exceptions.

Liberty and Privacy Are Alive and Well

The review court's decision does not lighten by one iota the government's burden of showing—before it can use FISA to wiretap you, me, the neighborhood drug dealer, or the Muslim family down the street—that the target is an agent of a foreign terrorist group or government. And the definition of a foreign "agent" includes U.S. citizens only when there is evidence implicating them in conduct that crosses the line of criminality or comes very close to it: "sabotage or international terrorism," which are crimes; activities "in preparation therefor"; or "clandestine intelligence-gathering activities [that] involve or may involve a [criminal] violation."

It's true that this decision clears the way for more wiretaps and searches, because the government can now use FISA when its primary purpose is prosecution. But critics are quite wrong to suggest that this opens the way for FISA surveillance to seek evidence of *ordinary* crimes. Few criminals or suspects are foreign agents. And the review court *rejected* the administration's argument that the USA-PATRIOT Act authorized use of FISA to seek to implicate foreign agents in ordinary crimes.

"FISA as amended is constitutional," the review court ruled, "because the surveillances it authorizes are reasonable."

Chapter 4

What Challenges Will the Espionage and Intelligence-Gathering Community Face in the Twenty-First Century?

Chapter Preface

Intelligence-gathering agencies face many challenges in the twenty-first century, including how to employ advanced technology. For example, some authorities argue that the United States should move from manned spy aircraft to unmanned satellite intelligence in order to prevent the kind of catastrophe that occurred near China in 2001. In April of that year, a Chinese pilot forced down an American EP-3, a propeller-driven reconnaissance aircraft. Unlike the U-2, used for reconnaissance during the Cold War, the EP-3 does not fly over hostile territory but collects communications and other signals intelligence from the edges of hostile nations. Unfortunately, these slower, low-flying intelligence-gathering aircraft are easy targets for antiaircraft missiles and fighter planes. According to journalist James Hackett, "The vulnerability of the planes and the possibility of their crews becoming hostages is an incentive to find a better way to collect intelligence." Hackett suggests that the United States get its intelligence with the technology already available—satellites in space.

Other commentators are concerned that using satellites to gather intelligence would threaten civil liberties. Some claim that satellites are already being used to spy on American citizens. In 1948 the U.S. National Security Agency (NSA) created a global spy system, code-named ECHELON, in cooperation with the United Kingdom, Canada, Australia, and New Zealand. Stations positioned in these and other nations capture satellite, microwave, cellular, and fibre-optic communications. After being decoded by NSA computers, analysts forward flagged messages to the intelligence agencies that request them. According to Patrick S. Poole, deputy director of the Center for Technology Policy, beyond intercepting messages from terrorists and rogue states, ECHELON is being used in "the regular discovery of domestic surveillance targeted at American civilians for reasons of 'unpopular' political affiliation or for no probable cause at all—in violations of the First, Fourth, and Fifth Amendments of the U.S. Constitution."

American intelligence agencies, however, deny such accusations. "We are not out there as a vacuum cleaner," claims former NSA Director Michael Hayden. "We don't have that capability and we don't want that capability." These agencies also deny that they violate privacy laws. "We protect the rights of Americans and their privacy," claims CIA Director George Tenet. "We do not violate them and we never will." Many agency advocates argue that congressional actions in the 1970s led to sufficient protections of Americans' privacy. Congress barred intelligence agencies from conducting surveillance against American citizens after the NSA admitted that it had used massive eavesdropping equipment to spy on anti–Vietnam War activists such as Jane Fonda and Benjamin Spock during the 1970s. In 1978 Congress passed the Foreign Intelligence Surveillance Act, which requires a special court order to authorize electronic surveillance of U.S. citizens. Some congressional leaders remain concerned, however. According to congressman Bob Barr, "It is difficult, if not impossible, to argue that laws written in the 1970s are adequate for today's intelligence challenges."

Authorities continue to debate whether spy satellites will protect citizens or violate their civil liberties. The authors in the following chapter examine this and other challenges faced by intelligence-gathering agencies in the twenty-first century.

The Changing Nature of Warfare Requires New Intelligence-Gathering Techniques

by G.I. Wilson, John P. Sullivan, and Hal Kempfer

About the authors: *G.I. Wilson is a U.S. Marine Corps Reserve colonel, John P. Sullivan is a sergeant in the Los Angeles County Sheriff's Department, and Hal Kempfer is a U.S. Marine Corps Reserve lieutenant colonel.*

Our world and the nature of conflict are changing. The ways we wage war and protect the public are also rapidly changing. The now-and-future conflict is transnational and global; it includes the American homeland and cyberspace and attacks on civilians.

Fourth-Generation Warfare

This "fourth-generation warfare" is manifesting itself in highly compartmentalized, cellular, predatory adversaries operating in networks outside the framework of traditional nation-states.

Urban operations, crime, and terrorism are now part of the same operational environment. We are witnessing them emerging and mutating into new forms of warfare, blurring distinctions between crime and war. Fourth-generation warfare (4GW) moves beyond terrorism, suggesting that terrorism will take advantage of that type of warfare's three main characteristics: the loss of the nation-state's monopoly on war; a return to a world of cultures and nation-states in conflict; and internal segmentation or division along ethnic, religious, and special-interest lines within our own society.

On 11 September 2001, an unthinkable fourth-generation idea moved from the realm of the potential into the realm of reality. In a surprisingly graphic, coordinated, nearly simultaneous attack on the World Trade Center in New York and the Pentagon in Washington, DC, the scourge of global networked terrorism brutally assaulted the American homeland.

These attacks mirrored the rage of criminals who use violence with perceived impunity to secure political and social ends. Distinctions between military and civilian were suspended as a result of the nature of targets chosen by al Qaeda [the terrorist group responsible for the attacks]. We now face a fourth-generation opponent without a nation-state base.

Our new adversaries are diverse and linked in unfamiliar ways. Loose coalitions of criminal actors, guerrillas, and insurgents who operate outside the nation-state now challenge national security capabilities that were designed to operate within a nation-state framework. Beyond that framework, our traditional structures have great difficulties engaging such threats.

As Martin van Creveld noted in *The Transformation of War*, throughout most of man's time on earth war has been non-trinitarian. Families waged war, as did clans, tribes, cities, monastic orders, religions, and even commercial enterprises (e.g., the British East India Company). They fought for many reasons other than for the state—croplands, loot, women, slaves, victims to sacrifice to their gods, and even for the purity of their race. Often there was no formal army with ranks and uniforms set apart from the people: every male strong enough to carry a weapon was a warrior.

A Continuous Conflict

War and crime are increasingly intertwined, yielding ethnic enmity, refugees, displaced persons, and opportunities for criminal exploitation. These conflicts are exploited and fueled by crime bosses, gang leaders, tribal chieftains, and warlords supported by non-state soldiers (gangs, clans, and mercenaries). This adds to the complexity of threats, blurring the lines among peace, war, and crime.

These recurring bad actors—criminals, irregular rogue bands, warring clans, and gangs—operate largely at the low end of the technological spectrum, yet, as we are increasingly seeing, they are beginning to exploit technology. The access to technology and cyberspace by bellicose factions is facilitated by money from organized crime. Transnational criminal organizations (TCOs) are networked more than ever and control large sums of money. It is not hard to imagine these entities going beyond their current co-option of governments to actually capturing a state (and its war-making capabilities) to further their goals.

> *"We now face a fourth-generation opponent without a nation-state base."*

The world of today and tomorrow is one dominated by conflict and random violence between the "haves" and the "have nots." Those with a conflicting cultural or religious ideology are likely to challenge our superiority according to their rules, not ours. Their modus operandi blur and will continue to blur the distinctions between crime and war, criminal and civil, combatant and non-combatant. Their actions will seek to exploit the seams of the modern state's internal and external security structures. These emerging challengers will embrace unconventional means not amenable to conventional responses.

Advanced technologies, once largely the sole domain of highly developed nation-states, are now finding their way into other hands and rogue nations. Technical sophistication is no longer limited to members of nation-states. High-tech applications for waging war—from advanced software simulation and GPS [Global Positioning System] data to high-resolution satellite imagery—are commercially available. Adaptive terrorist tactics are surfacing that are central to fourth-generation warfare.

> *"Those with a conflicting cultural or religious ideology are likely to challenge our superiority according to their rules, not ours."*

Post-modern conflict may be so ambiguous and diffuse that the conventional operational environment may all but disappear as a means of describing this setting of conflict. The distinction between "civilian" and military continues to erode and may—in many senses—disappear. Actions will occur concurrently throughout all participants' depth, including their society as a cultural, not just a physical, entity. Success will depend heavily on effectiveness in joint and coalition operations in a number of simultaneous theaters of operations, both outside the United States and domestically within the US, as lines between responsibility and mission become increasingly ambiguous.

Multiple Operating Environments

Fourth-generation warfare will be found in a variety of settings, spanning the spectrum of conflict from routine criminal activity and high-intensity crime through low- and mid-intensity conflict. Activities will often converge wherever one finds adversaries operating outside the conventions of the nation-state. For example, peacekeeping and peace-support operations humanitarian and consequence-management missions, counterterrorism, and counter-infowar missions may overlap, erupting in what former Marine Corps Commandant General Charles C. Krulak described in a prescient 1997 speech to the National Press Club as "Three-Block War."

Where the three blocks converge has been and will continue to be complicated by varying degrees of crime. Ethnic conflict is frequently exploited or exacerbated by organized crime and gangs to further their goals. Warlords and terrorists engage in drug trafficking to finance their campaigns. This complex mix places significant challenges and demands on individual military operators and civil police.

Blending civil protection, police, and combat skills demands a high degree of situational recognition and knowledge to understand which response is required and when it is required. Individuals or small units must become adept at this kind of decision-making, which presents large leadership challenges at all ranks. To support the complex range of activities required to navigate fourth-generation conflict adequate intelligence surveillance and reconnaissance (including cultural intelligence and real-time active mapping and sensors) must be available to skilled operators who can adapt their tactics and the activities of small, independent-action forces to a variety of missions and circumstances.

The Needs of Intelligence

Intelligence is the foundation for determining the kind of war we might be entering and thwarting those who would undermine national and international security. Simply put: Intelligence needs to provide indications and warning (I&W) and human-source intelligence (HUMINT) needs to discover and discern the plans and intentions of terrorists, gangsters, warlords, and rogue regimes.

Sound intelligence is crucial. It must give us the clearest possible insights into situations, events, players, and hidden agendas, so our leaders can decide quickly how or even if to engage. Intelligence must be able to warn of any potential surprises a warfighter is likely to face.

Lack of situational awareness has long been recognized as a major impediment to executing appropriate courses of action. This shortfall applies not only to fourth-generation warfare and terrorism, but also to crisis and complex-incident management (i.e., peace operations, urban operations, counterterrorism, complex humanitarian emergencies, consequence management, and disaster response). We need to anticipate and understand the dynamics of these issues, having not only knowledge dominance but also, more importantly, dominance in understanding the context of the action, event, or engagement.

> *"Intelligence is the foundation for determining the kind of war we might be entering and thwarting those who would undermine national and international security."*

Consider the benefits of understanding the context in urban operations. For example, the influence of three-dimensional terrain features and density are vital pieces of information for a commander faced with executing a rescue mission, constabulary operation, or providing humanitarian assistance in a third world mega-city inhabited by gangs, criminal enclaves, and sprawling slums. A world of constant change demands flexibility from intelligence networks after realistic expectations have been established for intelligence-gathering operations. For intelligence personnel, adapting and improvising must be a way of life.

Conducting Urban Operations

Much of the potential battlespace of the future will be urban. US forces, as well as those of our allies, will conduct urban expeditionary operations against terrorists, paramilitaries, and gangsters linked to internationally networked organized crime. Some of these urban operations will be within the United States, supporting domestic law-enforcement and emergency-response agencies in coalition-type organizational settings.

As history has repeatedly demonstrated, urban operations are complex and brutal. Yet the current and future world landscape—not to mention our adversaries—will make urban operations unavoidable.

As the aftermath of the World Trade Center attack graphically demonstrates, urban settings are extremely complex. The urban battlescape or operational space possesses subterranean, surface, building, and rooftop features. Structures, subway tunnels, enclosed pedestrian bridges, trolley cars and trams with overhead power, roadways, alleys, sewers, tunnels and parking garages allow multiple avenues of approach, firing positions, and obstacles. Under the best of conditions, lines of sight are diminished, inhibiting sensors and communications capabilities. After a large bombing or collapse of a high-rise building, terrain recognition is further complicated.

In *Heavy Matter: Urban Operations Density of Challenges*, noted urban operations scholar Dr. Russell Glenn observed that complexity is a feature of all urban operations. Among the factors noted are compressed decision times, increased operational tempo, and thousands, up to tens of thousands, of inhabitants per "cubic kilometer." These factors promise to degrade command and control, complicate decision-making, and challenge intelligence, surveillance, and reconnaissance efforts. Density, noise, and clutter make accurate, real-time situational awareness an elusive goal.

The military and urban civil protection and emergency services (police and fire service) stand to gain much by working together to better understand the urban environment. As the Russians recently relearned in Chechnya, urban operations are extremely demanding and taxing. The World Trade Center attacks demonstrated the complexity of the urban environment in a modern, western megalopolis. Our military, police, and fire service will have to operate together in this urban environment to protect the public and counter terrorist criminals as the Fourth Generation continues to unfold.

Intelligence Is Everyone's Business

A new intelligence paradigm needs to be crafted that acknowledges realistic expectations for intelligence-related activities and specifies that intelligence is, in fact, everyone's business. Forging this capability will require a definition of the threat environment, collaboration among the military services and a variety of actors (including the intelligence community and non-traditional players such as law-enforcement agencies), experimentation and, finally, implementation.

New tools and approaches are needed to sort pertinent information from noise. In addition, we must illuminate the mission-essential tasks of potential adversaries by exploiting both traditional and nontraditional tools and the information infrastructure through better use of open-source intelligence (OSINT), deception, and development of cyber-intelligence (CyberINT). HUMINT is an essential element of this approach. Combining traditional tools, HUMINT, OSINT, and CyberINT can assist in identifying the precursors and indicators of violence (such as group mobilization, criminal ex-

> *"A new intelligence paradigm needs to be crafted that acknowledges . . . that intelligence is, in fact, everyone's business."*

ploitation, and proliferation of materials for weapons of mass destruction) that may trigger a military (or a combined military-civil) response. Adopting the concept of "Deep I&W," that is, extending sensing to capture emerging trends and potentials prior to recognition of an overt threat to minimize the foe's advantage, is essential. To do so, sensing, surveillance, and reconnaissance efforts will require a flexible, integrated analysis and synthesis component.

Building New Teams

Meeting fourth-generation warfare threats to stability and security requires a direct and enduring commitment to forward-thinking military and civil readiness. While many new skills and interagency linkages are needed, efforts to build homeland defense will not require a cold start. On the operational and intelligence front, innovative structures, such as the Los Angeles Terrorism Early Warning (TEW) Group, have been bringing together emergency responders from law enforcement, the fire service, DoD [Department of Defense] entities, and the medical and public health communities to provide indications and warning and operational net assessments for several years.

The TEW model is a hybrid form, combining the attributes of networked organization to the traditionally hierarchical emergency-response disciplines. By integrating military support to civil authorities into its on-going efforts, the TEW can speed the process of accepting follow-on military assistance and draw upon military planning skills (from local military entities such as the USMC at Camp Pendleton, California National Guard, 9th Civil Support Teams) to enhance its process.

The TEW model involves collaboration among local, state, and federal law-enforcement and response agencies. It is designed to provide the operational intelligence needed to quickly develop potential courses of action, move through the decision cycle, forecast potential events, and craft meaningful courses of action for interagency interdisciplinary response.

Collaboration and partnership, such as interagency, interdisciplinary partnerships with law-enforcement agencies to explore and experiment with novel intelligence applications and approaches for the emerging threat environment should be explored. We need to focus sharply on what lies ahead seeking ideas about emerging and future conflict. We need to further develop and integrate our open-source intelligence, HUMINT, and cultural intelligence capabilities. To meet the threat of "now and future" warfare, our intelligence must focus more on cultural and social paradigms, not just military orders of battle.

Our adversaries span the globe. We face a shifting constellation of bad actors, competitors, sometimes-allies, non-combatants, and criminal opportunists. We will meet them in settings ranging from humanitarian stability and support operations to terrorist attacks, consequence management for complex emergencies, and ethno-religious cultural violence.

To be sure, our world and the nature of conflict are changing. The ways we wage war and protect the public are also rapidly changing. We are witnessing emerging and mutating forms of warfare, embodied by the blurring of crime and war, decline of the nation-state, increasingly lethal terrorism, and the manifestation of highly compartmentalized, cellular, predatory, networked adversaries.

We must learn from our experiences to adapt and develop news intelligence applications and approaches to these emerging and evolving fourth-generation threats at the intersection of crime and war. And we must do so quickly, because fourth-generation warfare is already here.

Emerging Terrorist Threats Require New Spying Strategies

by Gregory F. Treverton

About the author: *Gregory F. Treverton is senior policy analyst at the RAND Corporation, senior fellow at the Pacific Council on International Policy, and author of the book* Reshaping National Intelligence for an Age of Information.

The old and new worlds of intelligence met on September 11, 2001, when terrorists attacked the World Trade Center and the Pentagon.

Terrorism is an old-world problem in new-world circumstances. The new world is much more open, with vast amounts of information, much of which is neither owned by US intelligence agencies nor can be regarded as reliable—for example, that stew of fact, fiction, and disinformation known as the Web.

Openness needs to be put at the heart of the intelligence business. Exploiting secrets used to be the stock in trade of intelligence. But now the task is wider: gathering and sifting through a flood of information. This changed world requires a fundamental reshaping of the intelligence business.

Terrorists, however, are not part of the new openness. They do not advertise their plans, so the intelligence agencies' special sources are still important—espionage, or human intelligence (HUMINT), intercepted communications or other signals (SIGINT), and photos or other images (IMINT). Yet, even to grapple with terrorism, methods from the old world need to be reshaped by the circumstances of the new.

New Methods of Spying

The CIA needs to conduct espionage in a very new way—more tightly targeted and operating mostly independent of US embassies abroad. Spying will also have to be a more "cooperative" venture. American spy-masters will seldom be able to crack into terrorist cells, but other countries, including those that are not friends of the United States, may be more able to do so. Already, US intelligence is working with Sudan, despite its inclusion on Washington's list of terrorist sponsors.

Spying is most valued for solving immediate, tactical puzzles—such as, what is [terrorist] Osama bin Laden planning? These puzzles have a solution, if only we had access to the information. Puzzles were intelligence's stock-in-trade during the cold war: How many missiles does the Soviet Union have? How accurate are they? What is Iraq's order of battle?

> *"This changed world requires a fundamental reshaping of the intelligence business."*

Puzzles' opposites are mysteries, questions that have no answer even in principle: Will North Korea keep its part of the nuclear bargain? Will China's Communist Party cede primacy? What will Mexico's inflation rate be this year? The mystery can only be illuminated; it cannot be "solved."

Spying, however, is a target-of-opportunity enterprise. What spies may hear or steal today, or be able to communicate to their American case officers today, they may not hear or see or be able to get out tomorrow. What is decisive today may be unobtainable tomorrow. Worse, the crisis moments when information from spies is most valuable to us may be precisely when they are most exposed, when to communicate with them is to run the greatest risk of disclosing their connection to us.

Secrets are more valuable with regard to enduring puzzles, ones that will still matter tomorrow if they are not solved today. A foreigner's negotiating position is a perishable secret; after today's round, the US negotiator will know it. By contrast, the order of battle for the Iraqi military is an enduring puzzle: Whatever we know today, another puzzle piece will always be welcome tomorrow.

Reshaping the CIA

The required reshaping of the CIA's clandestine service, the spy-masters, goes well beyond what is imaginable in today's political climate. Indeed, today's first answer—more money—is exactly what is not required.

First, espionage should be narrowed to focus on potential foes of US troops abroad, the governments of a small number of potentially destabilizing states, and groups that threaten terrorist activities against the US.

Second, this streamlining means that the CIA would no longer have stations everywhere around the globe. There is merit to the counterargument—that our untidy world makes it impossible to predict where the US will want to act, and so some infrastructure for spying should be sustained almost everywhere. But on balance, the risk of such a far-flung presence outweighs the gain.

Third, the reshaped clandestine service would operate from the US and through case officers abroad, outside embassies, under nonofficial cover. Operating under official cover is paper thin in any case; what it mostly supplies is diplomatic immunity, thus lowering the risk to CIA spies, should they be caught by local counterintelligence.

During the cold war, when the CIA's targets were Soviet officials anywhere and officials and politicians from the local country, the diplomatic cocktail-party circuit was not a bad place to troll for recruits. But terrorists or Colombian drug-cartel leaders aren't likely guests on the embassy circuit.

Cracking the hardest targets, like terrorist cells, is a very painstaking and chancy business. Other countries, those closer to the terrorist organizations, including countries that are not US "friends," may have better luck. The US will need to work with them.

U.S. Counterintelligence Methods Must Be Improved

by Richard Shelby

About the author: *Richard Shelby, a Republican senator from Alabama, serves as chairman of the U.S. Senate Select Committee on Intelligence.*

Spying has been described as the world's "second oldest profession"—and one that is, in the words of one former CIA official, "just as honorable as the first."

Espionage has been with us since Moses sent agents to spy out the land of Canaan and the Philistines sent Delilah to assess Samson's vulnerabilities. And spies are with us today. I will not attempt to cover the history of espionage from Biblical days to now, but I would like to take the opportunity to address some important recent history, and lessons from recent history, as well as some of the issues and challenges, new and old, that we face as we address counterintelligence in the 21st century.

Let me emphasize at the outset that due to the extremely sensitive nature of the subject, and the fact that some of the matters I will discuss are the subject of ongoing investigations, I will be speaking for the most part in very general terms.

The first point I would like to make is that, as those of you who follow counterintelligence are well aware, between the peaks of public attention that attend the arrest of an [Aldrich] Ames, [a spy within the CIA], or a [Robert Philip] Hanssen, [a spy within the FBI], or a case like the Wen Ho Lee case, [in which Lee was accused of selling nuclear secrets to China], there is a quiet but steady parade of espionage or espionage-related arrests and convictions.

A July 1997 Defense Security Service publication lists more than 120 cases of espionage or espionage-related activities against the United States from 1975 to 1997. And those are just the ones that got caught.

Since then, we have had the Peter Lee case; the [Theresa Marie] Squillacote and [George] Trofimoff cases; David Boone, an NSA [National Security Agency] employee; Douglas Groat, who pled guilty to extortion against the CIA in a plea bargain in which espionage charges were dropped; the conviction

Richard Shelby, "Intelligence and Espionage in the Twenty-First Century," *Heritage Lectures*, May 18, 2001.

of INS [Immigration and Naturalization Service] official Mariano Faget of spying for Cuba; and, of course, the Hanssen case. Counterintelligence success or failure is often a matter of lessons learned or not learned. For today's purposes, I would like to concentrate on some lessons from the most damaging and high-profile . . . cases: Ames, PRC [Peoples Republic of China] espionage against our nuclear and missile programs, and the Hanssen case.

A Counterintelligence Disaster

In its investigation of the Ames case, the Senate Intelligence Committee found a counterintelligence disaster. Elements of this disaster included: a crippling lack of coordination between the CIA and the FBI, fundamental cultural and organizational problems in the CIA's counterintelligence organization, a willful disregard of Ames's obvious suitability problems, failure to coordinate and monitor Ames's contacts with Soviet officials, failure to restrict Ames's assignments despite early indications of anomalies, deficiencies in the polygraph program, deficiencies in the control of classified information, and coordination between the CIA's security and counterintelligence operations. Most disturbing was the CIA's failure to pursue an aggressive, structured, and sustained investigation of the catastrophic compromises resulting from Ames's espionage, in particular the destruction of the CIA's Soviet human asset program as a result of Ames's 1985 and 1986 disclosures.

By 1986, it was clear to the CIA that, as the SSCI [Senate Select Committee on Intelligence] report on the Ames matter concluded, "virtually its entire stable of Soviet assets had been imprisoned or executed." Yet as a result of the failure to mount an effective counterintelligence effort, it was another eight years before Ames was arrested. The FBI, which lost two of its most important assets following Ames's June 1985 disclosures, also bore responsibility for the failure to mount an adequate counterintelligence effort, as a 1997 report by the Department of Justice Inspector General made clear.

These two FBI assets, who were KGB officers, and a third KGB asset were betrayed by Hanssen in October 1985—just a few months after all three names were disclosed by Ames, according to the Justice Department affidavit in the Hanssen case. The

> *"Most disturbing was the CIA's failure to pursue an aggressive . . . and sustained investigation of the catastrophic compromises resulting from Ames's espionage."*

two KGB officers were later executed; the third asset was arrested and imprisoned. Also extremely disturbing, from my perspective, was the egregious failure by both the CIA and FBI, over the course of Ames's espionage, to inform the congressional oversight committees, despite the clear statutory obligation to notify the committees of "any significant intelligence failure."

While the committees obviously would not have been in a position to investigate the compromises themselves, they would certainly have exerted pressure that would have resulted in greater management attention and a more sustained effort that could have led to a more expeditious resolution.

Before leaving the Ames matter, I should point out that failure also may come from learning the wrong lessons. Most notably, many of the CIA's failings in the Ames case can be traced to an overreaction to the "excesses" of the [James Jesus] Angleton years, which thoroughly discredited the CIA's counterintelligence program, particularly in the Soviet-East European Division of the Directorate of Operations, where Ames worked.

China Steals Nuclear Secrets

Turning next to Chinese espionage against the Department of Energy [DOE] and U.S. nuclear weapons programs: unlike in the Ames case, extensive investigations into the compromise of U.S. nuclear weapons information have failed to resolve all the key questions.

That there was espionage, there is no doubt. As the April 1999 Intelligence Community Damage Assessment of PRC nuclear espionage concluded, "China obtained by espionage classified US nuclear weapons information." What is not yet known is how, and from whom, the Chinese got this information. As a result, we do not know enough of the story to attempt a final or definitive exercise in counterintelligence "lessons learned."

At the same time, a great deal is known about the overall security and

> *"Despite the history of espionage . . . the Department of Energy's counterintelligence program did 'not even meet minimal standards.'"*

counterintelligence problems at the DOE labs, which have been amply documented, for example in the report of the President's Foreign Intelligence Advisory Board. Because this is so well known, I will not touch upon it in detail, but will only make a few general observations. First, despite the history of espionage against the nuclear labs—and the obvious value of U.S. nuclear information to any nuclear power, whether established, emerging or aspiring—the Department of Energy's counterintelligence program did "not even meet minimal standards," in the words of the director of the program in November 1998.

He testified that "there is not a counterintelligence [program], nor has there been one at DOE for many, many years." This was a terrible failure of counterintelligence analysis and practice—and of common sense.

Moving from DOE to the role of the FBI, it is abundantly clear that the FBI counterintelligence investigation into the W-88 compromise lacked resources, motivation, and senior management attention; failed to pursue all relevant avenues of potential compromise; and was characterized by a number of missed opportunities. The CIA, for its part, failed to assign adequate priority or resources to the translation of the documents provided by the now-famous walk-in source.

But let me be clear: While the investigation and prosecution of Wen Ho Lee that emerged from the W-88 investigation have been widely criticized, we should not lose sight of the facts. Dr. Lee illegally, purposefully, downloaded and removed from [the] Los Alamos [National Laboratory, a nuclear research facility in New Mexico], massive amounts of classified nuclear weapons information—the equivalent of 400,000 pages of nuclear secrets, representing the fruits of 50 years and hundreds of billions of dollars worth of research. Now I would like to address the Hanssen case.

Investigating the Hanssen Case

Robert Philip Hanssen was arrested on February 18, [2001]. On March 5, the Senate Intelligence Committee directed the Department of Justice Inspector General to conduct a review of the Hanssen matter. On March 7, the Committee authorized a separate Committee investigation. Because of the ongoing criminal investigation and pending prosecution, I cannot go into details of Hanssen's alleged activities beyond what has already been made public by the FBI and the Department of Justice.

By the way, there is a great deal of information in that affidavit—too much information, some have suggested—and for anyone interested in counterintelligence, it is a fascinating and chilling story. Because there is much that is not yet known about this case, it would be premature for me to offer any definitive comments or lessons learned.

What I will do is identify some of the questions and issues the Committee is investigating, and offer a few preliminary and personal observations.

First the Committee will prepare a factual summary of the Hanssen case outlining his FBI career and alleged espionage activities. An important question here, since the Justice Department affidavit describes only espionage activities from 1985 through 1991, and 1999 through February 2001, is explaining what may or may not have been an eight-year gap in Hanssen's activities.

We also need to know if he was involved in any activities of concern prior to 1985. The Committee will examine whether there were counterintelligence warning flags indicating a penetration of the FBI—for example, source reporting or unexplained compromises of human sources or technical programs—and the response of the counterintelligence community, if any, to these events.

"How did the nation's premier counterintelligence organization fail to detect a spy in its midst for 15 years?"

This is a critical issue. The 1997 Department of Justice Inspector General report on the Ames case criticized the FBI for failing to mount an intensive counterintelligence effort to pursue evidence of catastrophic damage to the FBI's and CIA's Russian operations beginning in 1985.

The signs were there, but the FBI did not pursue them in an aggressive and systematic fashion. We now know that such an effort might have detected Hanssen, as well. We will look closely at the FBI's efforts following the 1997 IG [Inspector General] report to see if the agency applied these lessons from the Ames investigation to its ongoing counterintelligence efforts.

There have been press reports of other source information or counterintelligence analyses that might have pointed to Hanssen sooner. I cannot address those reports; I can only say that we are reviewing both Ames-era and post-Ames reporting and analysis to determine whether any relevant warning flags were missed.

Moving to Hanssen himself, the Committee will review possible warning flags in Hanssen's own behavior that raised, or should have raised, questions about his loyalty or suitability, and the response, if any, by Hanssen's colleagues and security personnel.

FBI internal security procedures during the period of Hanssen's activities will be another critical focus of the Committee's work. The Committee will review personnel security issues, such as the FBI's failure to adopt an across-the-board polygraph program comparable to those at the CIA and NSA, and the adequacy of financial disclosure requirements.

> *"The drafters of ["Counterintelligence for the 21st Century"] found current U.S. counterintelligence capabilities to be 'piecemeal and parochial.'"*

The Committee will look hard at the FBI's computer and information systems security practices, and at Hanssen's computer activities, including the possibility that he gained unauthorized access or might have manipulated FBI computer systems. Another issue is the control of classified information in general. Hanssen appears to have been able to gain authorized or unauthorized access to an extremely wide range of sensitive intelligence programs and activities, many of which may have been beyond his "need to know." (Ames too was able to gain access to a great deal of information for which he had no need to know.)

This problem may be FBI-wide, and not limited to Hanssen. In the 1987 ANLACE report—the first of several inconclusive efforts to solve the 1985 Ames/Hanssen compromises I described earlier—FBI agents found that as many as 250 FBI employees in the Washington Field Office alone had knowledge of these highly sensitive cases. Also, I am concerned that Hanssen was able, according to the affidavit, to provide the KGB with original documents (rather than copies), pointing to a serious failure in document control.

These security issues also are the subject of Judge [William] Webster's investigation. We look forward to the results of the Webster Commission, which should aid the Committee in making budgetary and other decisions to enhance security at the FBI.

The impact of Hanssen's alleged espionage on operational, budgetary, and programmatic decisions across the Intelligence Community goes to the heart of the Committee's responsibilities and will be a critical component of our review. The key issues include: what operations, programs and sources were compromised, and their remaining utility, if any; how much it will cost to replace or replicate these capabilities, if it can be done at all; and the impact of the compromise on the utility of these collection capabilities against other, non-Russian targets. The Committee will review the possibility that Moscow used sources or programs compromised by Hanssen for "perception management" purposes.

> *"An agent can transfer or simply retype classified information into an unclassified e-mail system and send it around the world in seconds."*

In the wake of the Ames case, the CIA concluded that the Soviets and later the Russians had used controlled sources or information compromised by Ames to manipulate U.S. assessments of issues ranging from internal Soviet political developments to Soviet and Russian military capabilities and Russian policy toward the former Soviet republics.

In sum, the Committee will collect the facts, identify shortcomings and failures in the FBI's internal security and counterintelligence operations that may have facilitated Hanssen's alleged activities, determine the impact on the U.S. government's intelligence collection efforts, and take such legislative or other steps as appropriate.

The Committee also will review possible changes in law to facilitate the investigations and prosecution of espionage cases. This process may take some time, as the final assessment of the Hanssen case will not be completed for some time, even if Hanssen were to reach a plea agreement tomorrow. In the meantime, we intend to take preliminary steps, as appropriate, in this year's intelligence authorization bill.

Difficult Questions About Hanssen

Let me offer a few general thoughts on the Hanssen matter, reiterating that these are personal and preliminary in nature. First, let me restate the obvious question: How did the nation's premier counterintelligence organization fail to detect a spy in its midst for 15 years? While a number of explanations have been and will continue to be offered, it is difficult to avoid returning to that simple question. In any case, we intend to find out the answer. Part of the answer may lie in Hanssen's ability to use his knowledge of FBI activities and techniques to avoid detection.

While some of the early assessments of Hanssen as a master spy may have been exaggerated, it is clear that he was in a position to benefit from his inside knowledge of FBI procedures, and that would explain at least some of his success in evading detection for so long. On the other hand, it seems fair to say that

Hanssen, like Ames, benefited from the FBI's failure aggressively to pursue the source of the 1985 agent losses and other compromised FBI activities, as documented by the Justice Department IG.

Second, why didn't the FBI do more to take advantage of the lessons that the CIA learned so painfully from the Ames case with respect to financial disclosure, compartmentation, an effective polygraph program, and other security and counterintelligence measures? Granted, the reforms adopted by the CIA post-Ames could not have stopped Hanssen in time to prevent grave damage to the national security because Ames's arrest and the subsequent recriminations and reforms came almost a decade after Hanssen appears to have started spying. On the other hand, we may well learn that additional losses could in fact have been avoided had Hanssen been caught five years earlier.

> *"[One] challenge . . . is the difficulty of protecting sensitive, proprietary, or even classified information in the course of scientific exchange."*

A Restructured National Counterintelligence System

I would now like to move to an important development in national-level counterintelligence policy.

On December 28, 2000, President [Bill] Clinton signed a Presidential Decision Directive entitled "U.S. Counterintelligence Effectiveness—Counterintelligence for the 21st Century," or "CI-21." President [George W.] Bush has proceeded to implement the directive, CI-21 reflects the concerns of senior counterintelligence officials—which the Committee shared—over the ability of existing U.S. counterintelligence structures, programs, and policies to address both emerging threats and traditional adversaries using cutting-edge technologies and tradecraft in the 21st century. I am pleased to say that the Senate Intelligence Committee, on a bipartisan basis, played an important role in keeping the pressure on the executive branch to force them to come up with a counterintelligence reform plan even when the executive branch process bogged down amid interagency disagreements.

From an analytical perspective, CI-21 restates and expands upon other recent assessments of the emerging counterintelligence environment. It recognizes that the threat has expanded beyond the traditional paradigm of "adversary states stealing classified data"—which includes traditional espionage by Russia, the PRC, and others—to include new efforts by these traditional adversaries, as well as certain allies and friendly states, to collect economic information and critical but sometimes unclassified technologies, as we have just seen in the Lucent case [in which three Lucent scientists were accused of selling trade secrets to a Chinese government-owned company].

A key element of this threat is the growing use of modern technology, particularly modern computer technology and the Internet, to develop information warfare (IW) and intelligence collection capabilities and intelligence tradecraft that alter traditional notions of time, distance, and access.

Faced by these emerging challenges, the drafters of the CI-21 plan found current U.S. counterintelligence capabilities to be "piecemeal and parochial," and recommended adoption of a new counterintelligence philosophy—described as more policy-driven, prioritized, and flexible, with a strategic, national-level focus.

CI-21 also established a restructured national counterintelligence system. Key elements of the plan include a proactive, analytically driven approach to identifying and prioritizing the information to be protected, enhanced information-sharing between counterintelligence elements, and more centralized guidance for counterintelligence policies and resources.

CI-21 proposes significant changes in the way the United States government approaches, and organizes itself to meet, the threat of foreign espionage and intelligence gathering. The Committee looks forward to working with the new Administration to ensure the effective implementation of the CI-21 plan.

Thinking the Unthinkable

In closing, I would like to make a couple of general points about the challenge of counterintelligence in the 21st century.

The first is the impact of technology. Modern microelectronics and information technology have revolutionized just about everything else, so it is not surprising they would have an impact on counterintelligence. After all, the currency of espionage is information. Therefore, the impact of evolving information technologies is particularly significant.

One aspect of this is the miniaturization of information. It took Jonathan Pollard, [a U.S. Navy intelligence analyst convicted of selling secrets to Israel], 17 months to spirit away enough classified documents to fill a 360 cubic foot room.

Today, that information can fit in a pocket, dramatically diminishing the risk of detection while increasing the productivity of an agent. A laptop computer like the one that disappeared from the State Department can fit into a briefcase or backpack yet yield an entire library of information.

Another is the revolutionary change in the dissemination of information. Depending on the computer security measures in place, an agent can transfer or simply retype classified information into an unclassified e-mail system and send it around the world in seconds.

Or consider the "virtual dead drop." No more marks on mail boxes or hiding messages in a soda can. Classified information can be transferred or retyped into an unclassified computer with an Internet connection, and left there for someone to "hack" into. The whole transaction may be difficult or impossible for security officials to detect or recreate. Even if the agent is careless and fails

> *"Thinking the unthinkable is not getting any easier, but it is just as critical to our national security."*

to delete classified information from an unclassified computer, it may be difficult if not impossible to prove anything beyond a security violation.

Another challenge, in an era of extensive scientific cooperation between nations that are, if not adversaries, not exactly friends, is the difficulty of protecting sensitive, proprietary, or even classified information in the course of scientific exchange or joint ventures. This problem was especially apparent in the
interactions between American and Chinese engineers launching U.S. satellites
in China that were the subject of an Intelligence Committee investigation.

American satellite company engineers, who have multimillion-dollar pay-
loads riding on primitive Chinese rockets, face a serious conflict of interest:
how to ensure successful launches while not doing anything to improve Chinese rockets that are essentially identical to Chinese ICBMs in everything but
the payload. Identifying sensitive, but unclassified, technical information at risk
in transactions of this type, and then finding ways to protect it, will be an important focus of the CI-21 plan.

Most fundamental to counterintelligence—as true today as ever—is the need
to "think the unthinkable." Yet this is one of the most difficult attitudes to instill
and maintain because it runs contrary to human nature, especially in open societies like the United States.

Consider the following scenarios: Two Soviet agents are named by an American President to serve as Secretary of State and Secretary of the Treasury.

Unthinkable? You might think so. Yet Henry Wallace, Vice President during
Franklin Roosevelt's third term, said later that if Roosevelt had died and he had
become President, he would have appointed Laurence Duggan and Harry Dex-
ter White—both of whom were revealed to have been Soviet agents—to those
positions. As it happened, Harry Truman replaced Wallace three months before
Roosevelt's death.

Or imagine that another Soviet agent became chief of the British Secret Intelligence Service, or SIS. Yet Kim Philby was one of the main contenders to take
over the SIS before he came under suspicion and eventually defected. (And
there are still people who claim that Roger Hollis, head of the British internal
security service MI-5, was a Soviet agent.)

Today, thinking the unthinkable is not getting any easier, but it is just as critical to our national security.

As we proceed to face the counterintelligence threat of the 21st century, we
are faced with a host of challenges: some new, others ancient and deeply rooted
in human weakness, and some not yet even invented.

I am pleased to say that today we have an Administration that is more willing
to see the world as it is, and not as we would wish it, and this gives me confidence in our ability to meet these challenges. I look forward to working with
the Bush Administration to build on the lessons of the past, and seize the opportunities of the present and future, to strengthen our national counterintelligence
policies and posture in defense of our nation's security.

Digital Spies Pose a Serious Threat to National Security

by Barry Neild

About the author: *Barry Neild is a British journalist who covers technology issues for publications such as* Computer Weekly.

When suburban granny Melita Norwood ambled down her garden path [in 1999] and proudly admitted to the assembled media that she had spent the best years of her life spying for the Soviet Government, it signalled the unearthing of a chapter of espionage history that had largely been buried under the remains of the Berlin Wall.

Mrs. Norwood's exposure as one of the spying game's more unlikely agents harked back to a nostalgia-steeped era of espionage—men in long coats meeting at midnight in rain-soaked railway stations, sotto voice conversations into Bakelite telephones, microfilms, poison-tipped umbrellas and the dusty, filing cabinet-lined corridors of Whitehall.

Norwood and the other spies are exposed in *The Sword and the Shield: The Mitrokhin Archive and the Secret History of the KGB*, an archive compiled by Soviet defector Vasill Mitrokhin—who smuggled out the secrets of the KGB in his socks.

Mitrokhin's method of data transfer highlights the extent to which this period has been eclipsed by the far more sinister sphere of electronic espionage. Digital spying has been heralded as much by the collapse of communism as by the arrival of such technological advancements as faxes, mobile phones and the Internet.

Abandoning Cloak and Dagger

Now the agents of espionage have abandoned their cloaks and daggers for computers that give them unlimited access to the World Wide Web. A good spy is no longer measured by their talent for slipping undetected across borders, but by their ability to crack the codes which offer entry into databases loaded with sensitive information.

The threat posed by these individuals is not to be taken lightly. No one realises this more than the US Government, which annually spends billions of dollars funding its own army of e-spies who sift through the vast global traffic of information passing through the Web.

Richard A Clarke, chairman of the US Government's chief counter-terrorism group, says that without adequate surveillance, the US is leaving itself open to an attack on the scale of an "electronic Pearl Harbour".

Earlier [in 1999] Clarke told the *New York Times*, "There is a real problem convincing people that there is a threat. Most people don't understand. Chiefs of big corporations don't even know what I'm talking

> *"Now the agents of espionage have abandoned their cloaks and daggers for computers that give them unlimited access to the World Wide Web."*

about. They think I'm talking about a 14-year-old hacking into their Web sites.

"I'm talking about people shutting down a city's electricity, 911 systems, telephone networks and transportation systems. You black out a city, people die. Black out lots of cities, lots of people die. It's as bad as being attacked by bombs.

"An attack on American cyberspace is an attack on the United States, just as much as a landing on New Jersey. The notion that we could respond with military force against a cyber-attack has to be accepted."

Evidence of the extent of this paranoia can be found, not in the technology-rich boulevards of Silicon Valley, but on remote moorland in North Yorkshire, [Great Britain], that is more James Herriott, [who writes stories about an English veterinarian living in the country], than James Bond.

Until recently, RAF [Royal Air Force] Menwith Hill was not marked on any map or mentioned in any guide to the RAF. Officially, the biggest electronic surveillance centre in the world does not exist. But drive along the A59 north of Harrogate, [Great Britain], and you cannot fail to notice 20 golf ball-shaped antennae, stretching out over 562 acres.

Questioning the Use of Surveillance

This parasitic presence on the hard shoulder of the Superhighway has not gone without criticism. An EU [European Union] report published earlier [in 1999] . . . laid bare the fact that US intelligence agents are able to read millions of confidential e-mails and other messages sent over the Internet. And it highlighted the fear that the information may be used for commercial espionage to give US companies an unfair advantage over their European rivals.

These "golf balls" feed the US National Security Agency (NSA) with the raw details of every electronic communication, ranging from highly sensitive commercial data to the inconsequential electronic phemera.

The report urges European countries to develop extra security for software used on PCs in a bid to thwart any attempt by security agents to crack their codes. It also warns that software in virtually every PC is designed to allow secure communications to be easily collected and deciphered by the NSA.

With this in mind, it came as no surprise when, several months later, a division of Microsoft was accused of leaving open a secret backdoor into its password-protected software—a claim the company firmly denied.

In Britain, both MI5, [the nation's domestic security intelligence agency], and MI6, [the nation's international Secret Intelligence Service (SIS)], now recruit e-spies via the Internet, and ideal candidates are more likely to be IT [information technology] workers than Oxbridge graduates.

Fictional spooks are also finally coming to terms with the spying game's new rules.

Whereas James Bond was once pitted against creepy bald blokes wearing Nehru jackets and stroking fluffy felines, in *Goldeneye* he faced corrupt computer whiz-kids who harassed our man by hunching over hardware and clattering keyboards.

Globalization Is Making It Easier for Foreign-Born Citizens to Spy on the United States

by Bill Gertz

About the author: *Bill Gertz is a defense and national security reporter for the* Washington Times. *He has also written articles for the* National Review *and* Weekly Standard *and is author of* Breakdown: How America's Intelligence Failures Led to September 11.

American spies are increasingly women and foreign-born citizens who succeed in passing secrets as volunteers, according to a Defense Department report on espionage.

About 20 Americans have committed espionage or tried to spy since 1990, the report states, and the globalization of economics and the information-technology revolution have made it difficult to stop government employees from giving away or selling secrets.

The Globalization of Espionage

"It does point to a kind of confluence of factors—the increase in the number of naturalized citizens, people who have foreign attachments and people who cite divided loyalty as a motive" for spying, said Katherine Herbig, co-author of the report, in an interview.

"These are all signs that the globalization we see going on is also happening in espionage."

Recent American spies "have been older, more likely to be women and more likely to be civilian" than in the past, she said. They are also more likely to be from an ethnic minority.

The report, "Espionage Against the United States by American Citizens 1947 to 2001," was produced by the Defense Personnel Security Research Center, a government think tank in Monterey, California, known as PERSEREC.

It surveyed 150 spy cases involving Americans and found that most spies in the past were white men in the military with little education.

"The end of the Cold War did not mean the end of espionage by Americans," the report stated, "but it seems to have brought changes in the practice of this crime."

Of the 20 spy cases since 1990, the report said, three involved spying by women and 11 involved Americans of an ethnic minority. Five of the spies from the 1990s, or 25 percent, were naturalized U.S. citizens for whom foreign attachments were a factor.

"The globalization of economics and the information-technology revolution have made it difficult to stop government employees from giving away or selling secrets."

The survey compared the spies of the 1990s with two groups of spies in earlier periods: The 65 spies uncovered between 1947 and 1979, and the 65 spies caught between 1980 and 1989, the so-called decade of the spy.

"American spies of the 1990s have been older, with a median age of 39, than either of the two earlier groups," the report said. "They include a larger proportion of women (15 percent), of racial and ethnic minorities, notably the 25 percent who were Hispanic Americans, and a lower proportion of married persons."

The increase in female spies is significant because out of 150 spies uncovered since 1947, 11 were women. The report noted that 10 of the 11 women spies worked as accomplices or partners of men.

The report was written before the discovery of a longtime spy within the Defense Intelligence Agency, Ana Belen Montes, who spied for Cuba for 10 years before being arrested in September 2001.

The Success of the New Spies

Reflecting an apparent decline of counterintelligence efforts, the report stated that 1990s spies were more successful than those in the '80s, when up to 45 percent of them were stopped before providing secrets to foreign nations.

Recent spies were successful in passing secrets four out of five times.

The vast majority of espionage cases since 1947 involved the Soviet Union and Russia, with a total of 114 out of 150 espionage cases involving Moscow or its Soviet bloc allies.

Among the other nations identified as "recipient countries" of American spies since 1947 were China, Cuba, the Philippines, Egypt, South Africa, Poland, East Germany, North Korea, France, Hungary, Czechoslovakia, Libya, Ecuador, Japan, Vietnam, Liberia, South Korea, Greece, Britain, the Netherlands, Israel, Saudi Arabia, Ghana, El Salvador, Jordan, Iraq and Taiwan.

The report states that naturalized American spies with "foreign attachments"—relatives abroad, emotional ties to foreign nations or overseas business ties—were more easily recruited by foreign intelligence services than those with no foreign ties.

Security vetting did not find people engaged in spying: At least five spies were not detected by screening and had clearances renewed while they committed espionage.

A key trend identified by the study was the "globalization" of economics, which is affecting the loyalty of Americans. Another was high-technology information systems. Spies' methods of collection, synthesis and transmission are changing, "shifting to take advantage of opportunities in these new technologies," the report said.

Organizations to Contact

The editors have compiled the following list of organizations concerned with the issues debated in this book. The descriptions are derived from materials provided by the organizations. All have publications or information available for interested readers. The list was compiled on the date of publication of the present volume; names, addresses, phone and fax numbers, and e-mail and Internet addresses may change. Be aware that many organizations take several weeks or longer to respond to inquiries, so allow as much time as possible.

American Center for Law and Justice (ACLJ)
PO Box 64429, Virginia Beach, VA 23467
(757) 226-2489 • fax: (757) 226-2836
website: www.aclj.org

The ACLJ is a nonprofit, public interest law firm committed to preventing the erosion of religious and civil liberties and dedicated to preserving freedom and democracy—rights it believes must be protected both domestically and internationally. The Center publishes articles and news reports on its website, including "FBI Reform: Can the Bureau Overcome the Bureaucracy?"

American Civil Liberties Union (ACLU)
125 Broad St., 18th Floor, New York, NY 10004-2400
(212) 549-2500
e-mail: aclu@aclu.org • website: www.aclu.org

The ACLU is a national organization that works to defend Americans' civil rights guaranteed by the U.S. Constitution, arguing that measures to protect national security should not compromise fundamental civil liberties. It publishes and distributes policy statements, pamphlets, and press releases with titles such as *Bigger Monster, Weaker Chains: The Growth of an American Surveillance Society*, which is available on its website.

Association of Former Intelligence Officers (AFIO)
6723 Whittier Ave., Suite 303A, McLean, VA 22101-4523
(703) 790-0320 • fax: (703) 790-0264
e-mail: afio@afio.com • website: www.afio.org

The AFIO is a group of former military and civilian intelligence officers who seek to educate the public on the role and importance of intelligence and the need for a strong and healthy U.S. intelligence/counterintelligence capability to protect U.S. citizens, to serve U.S. national interests, and for world stability. The AFIO publishes *Weekly Intelligence Notes* and the monthly *Periscope*, which is available on its website.

The Brookings Institution
1775 Massachusetts Ave. NW, Washington, DC 20036
(202) 797-6000 • fax: (202) 797-6004
e-mail: brookinfo@brook.edu • website: www.brookings.org

The Brookings Institution, founded in 1927, is a think tank that conducts research and education in foreign policy, economics, government, and the social sciences. Its National Security Council Project examines the council's importance in U.S. foreign policy and focuses on key issues relating to structure, policy, and interagency process. Other publications include books, the quarterly *Brookings Review*, periodic *Policy Briefs*, and commentary, including "How Operational and Visible an NSC?"

CATO Institute
1000 Massachusetts Ave. NW, Washington, DC 20001-5403
(202) 842-0200 • fax: (202) 842-3490
e-mail: cato@cato.org • website: www.cato.org

The institute is a nonpartisan public policy research foundation dedicated to limiting the role of government and protecting individual liberties. It publishes the quarterly magazine *Regulation*, the bimonthly *Cato Policy Report*, and numerous policy papers and articles. Works on intelligence include "Building Leverage in the Long War: Ensuring Intelligence Community Creativity," and "Why Spy? The Uses and Misuses of Intelligence."

Center for Defense Information
1779 Massachusetts Ave. NW, Suite 615, Washington, DC 20036
(202) 332-0600 • fax: (202) 462-4559
e-mail: info@cdi.org • website: www.cdi.org

The Center for Defense Information is a nonpartisan, nonprofit organization that researches all aspects of global security. It seeks to educate the public and policy makers about issues such as weapons systems, security policy, and defense budgeting. It publishes the monthly publication *Defense Monitor* and the *Weekly Defense Monitor*, which is available on its website.

Center for National Security Studies
1120 19th St. NW, 8th Floor, Washington, DC 20036
(202) 721-5650 • fax: (202) 530-0128
e-mail: cnss@gwu.edu • website: http://cnss.gwu/~cnss/center.htm

The Center for National Security Studies is a nongovernmental advocacy and research organization founded in 1974 to work for control of the FBI and CIA and to prevent violations of civil liberties. The center also works internationally to assist human rights organizations and government officials to establish oversight and accountability of intelligence agencies in emerging democracies. Its website explores issues related to government surveillance and intelligence oversight, including the Total Information Awareness program and FBI guidelines for investigations. The center publishes articles such as "Intelligence, Terrorism, and Civil Liberties," which is available on its website.

Central Intelligence Agency (CIA)
Office of Public Affairs, Washington, DC 20505
(703) 482-0623 • fax: (703) 482-1739
website: www.cia.gov

The CIA was created in 1947 with the signing of the National Security Act (NSA) by then-president Harry S. Truman. The NSA charged the Director of Central Intelligence (DCI) with coordinating the nation's intelligence activities and correlating, evaluating, and disseminating intelligence that affects national security. The CIA is an independent agency, responsible to the president through the DCI, and accountable to the American people through the Intelligence Oversight Committee of the U.S. Congress. Publications, including *Factbook on Intelligence* and *Report of Investigation—Volume II: The Contra Story*, are available on its website.

Federal Bureau of Investigation (FBI)
935 Pennsylvania Ave. NW, Room 7972, Washington, DC 20535
(202) 324-3000
website: www.fbi.gov

The FBI, the principal investigative arm of the U.S. Department of Justice, evolved from an unnamed force of special agents formed on July 26, 1908. It has the authority and responsibility to investigate specific crimes assigned to it. The FBI also is authorized to provide other law enforcement agencies with cooperative services, such as fingerprint identification, laboratory examinations, and police training. The mission of the FBI is to uphold the law through the investigation of violations of federal criminal law; to protect the United States from foreign intelligence and terrorist activities; to provide leadership and law enforcement assistance to federal, state, local, and international agencies; and to perform these responsibilities in a manner that is responsive to the needs of the public and is faithful to the Constitution of the United States. Press releases, congressional statements, and major speeches on issues concerning the FBI are available on the agency's website.

Federation of American Scientists (FAS)
1717 K St. NW, Washington, DC 20036
(202) 546-3300 • fax: (202) 675-1010
e-mail: fas@fas.org • website: www.fas.org

The FAS is a privately funded, nonprofit organization engaged in analysis and advocacy on science, technology, and public policy for global security. The FAS Intelligence Resource Program website includes official and unofficial resources on intelligence policy, structure, function, organization, and operations. The FAS publishes *Secrecy News*, an e-mail publication of the FAS Project on Government Secrecy that covers new developments in secrecy, security, and intelligence policies.

Hudson Institute Center on National Security Studies
Herman Kahn Center, 5395 Emerson Way, Indianapolis, IN 46226
(317) 545-1000 • fax: (317) 545-9639
e-mail: info@hudson.org • website: www.hudson.org

The Hudson Institute is an aggregate of policy research centers whose goal is to guide policy changes. The institute is committed to the free market and individual responsibility, confidence in technology to assist progress, and respect for the importance of culture and religion in human affairs. On its website, the Center on National Security Studies publishes commentary, reports, speeches, testimonies, and articles, including "High-Tech Antiterrorism and "A Colder War: Taking the Long View of the War on Terror."

Human Rights Watch
350 Fifth Ave., 34th Floor, New York, NY 10118-3299
(212) 290-4700 • fax: (212) 736-1300
e-mail: hrwnyc@hrw.org • website: www.hrw.org

Human Rights Watch monitors and reports human rights abuses in the United States and internationally. It sponsors fact-finding missions, disseminates results, and publishes the bimonthly *Human Rights Watch* newsletter. Information about the U.S. intelligence response to the September 11, 2001, terrorist attacks and its impact on human rights is available on its website, including articles such as "Foreign Enemies and Constitutional Rights" and the report, *Justice Undermined: Torture, Ill-Treatment, and Deaths in Custody.*

National Security Agency
9800 Savage Rd., Ft. Meade, MD 20755-6248
(301) 688-6524
website: www.nsa.gov

The National Security Agency coordinates, directs, and performs activities, such as designing cipher systems, which protect American information systems and produce foreign intelligence information. It is the largest employer of mathematicians in the United States and also hires the nation's best codemakers and codebreakers. Speeches, briefings, and reports are available on its website.

Privacy International
1718 Connecticut Ave. NW, Suite 200, Washington, DC 20009
(202) 483-1217 • fax: (202) 483-1248
e-mail: privacyint@privacy.org • website: www.privacy.org

Privacy International is an independent, nongovernment organization whose goal is to protect the privacy rights, threatened by increasing technology, of citizens worldwide. On its website, the organization provides archives of material on privacy, including international agreements, the report, *Freedom of Information and Access to Government Records Around the World*, and *Private Parts Online*, an online newsletter that reports recent stories on international privacy issues.

U.S. Department of State, Counterterrorism Office
Office of Public Affairs, Room 2507, 2201 C St. NW, Washington, DC 20520
(202) 647-4000
e-mail: secretary@state.gov • website: www.state.gov/s/ct

The office works to develop and implement American counterterrorism strategy and to improve cooperation with foreign governments. Articles and speeches by government officials are available on its website.

Bibliography

Books

James Bamford	*Body of Secrets: Anatomy of the Ultra-Secret National Security Agency from the Cold War Through the Dawn of a New Century.* New York: Doubleday, 2001.
Bruce Berkowitz and Allan E. Goodman	*Best Truth: Intelligence in the Information Age.* New Haven, CT: Yale University Press, 2000.
Alexander Cockburn and Jeffrey St. Clair	*Whiteout: The CIA, Drugs, and the Press.* New York: Verso Books, 1998.
John K. Cooley	*Unholy Wars: Afghanistan, America, and International Terrorism.* Sterling, VA: Pluto Press, 2002.
Craig Eisendrath, ed.	*National Insecurity: U.S. Intelligence After the Cold War.* Philadelphia: Temple University Press, 2000.
James Gannon	*Stealing Secrets, Telling Lies: How Spies and Codebreakers Helped Shape the Twentieth Century.* Washington, DC: Brassey's, 2001.
Ted Gup	*The Book of Honor: Covert Lives and Classified Deaths at the CIA.* New York: Doubleday, 2000.
Arthur Hulnick	*Fixing the Spy Machine: Preparing American Intelligence for the Twenty-First Century.* Westport, CT: Praeger, 1999.
Rhodri Jeffreys-Jones	*Cloak and Dollar: A History of American Secret Intelligence.* New Haven, CT: Yale University Press, 2002.
Loch K. Johnson	*Bombs, Bugs, Drugs, and Thugs: Intelligence and America's Quest for Security.* New York: New York University Press, 2002.
Mark M. Lowenthal	*Intelligence: From Secrets to Policy.* Washington, DC: CQ Press, 2000.
Stephen Paul Miller	*The Seventies Now: Culture as Surveillance.* Durham, NC: Duke University Press, 1999.
Jeffrey Richelson	*The U.S. Intelligence Community.* Boulder, CO: Westview Press, 1999.

Abram N. Shulsky and Gary J. Schmitt	*Silent Warfare: Understanding the World of Intelligence.* Washington, DC: Brassey's, 2002.
Athan G. Theoharis	*Chasing Spies: How the FBI Failed in Counterintelligence but Promoted the Politics of McCarthyism in the Cold War Years.* Chicago: Ivan R. Dee, 2002.
Gregory F. Treverton	*Reshaping National Intelligence for an Age of Information.* New York: Cambridge University Press, 2001.
Gary Webb	*Dark Alliance: The CIA, the Contras, and the Crack Cocaine Explosion.* New York: Seven Stories Press, 1998.
Amy B. Zegart	*Flawed by Design: The Evolution of the CIA, JCS, and NSC.* Stanford, CA: Stanford University Press, 1999.

Periodicals

Steven Aftergood	"Secrecy Is Back in Fashion," *Bulletin of the Atomic Scientists*, November 2000.
Gary Aldrich	"The FBI: Managing Disaster?" *Shield*, Spring 2002.
Russ Arensman	"Keeping Secrets," *Electronic Business*, May 2000.
Bruce Berkowitz	"Better Ways to Fix U.S. Intelligence," *Orbis*, Fall 2001.
Bruce Berkowitz	"Deep Cover," *Hoover Digest*, 2002.
Alexander Cockburn	"Total Information, Total Confusion," *Nation*, December 16, 2002.
Ralph De Toledano	"Ignoring Red Spies Is an Old, Old Story," *Insight*, August 23, 1999.
Dana Dillon	"Breaking Down Intelligence Barriers for Homeland Security," *Backgrounder*, April 15, 2002.
Uri Dowbenko	"Spooks, Whistleblowers, and Fall Guys," *Nexus*, August/September 1998.
Bruce Fein	"No License to Spy Indiscriminately," *Washington Times*, November 26, 2002.
Kendrick Frazier	"National Academy of Sciences Report Says Polygraph Testing Too Flawed for Security Screening," *Skeptical Inquirer*, January/February 2003.
Robert M. Gates	"The ABC's of Spying," *New York Times*, March 14, 1999.
Bill Gertz	"The FBI: The Decline of Domestic Intelligence," *World & I*, January 2003.
William Norman Grigg	"9/11: FBI Futility and Failure," *New American*, January 27, 2003.
Phillip G. Henderson	"Intelligence Gathering and September 11—What the Lessons of History Show," *World & I*, December 2002.
Sean D. Hill	"The Complexity of Intelligence Gathering," *Crime & Justice International*, October/November 2001.

Doug Ireland	"'New' FBI, Same Old Problems," *In These Times*, July 8, 2002.
William F. Jasper	"Watching Your Every Move," *New American*, January 27, 2003.
Scott Johnson	"Better Unsafe than (Occasionally) Sorry?" *American Enterprise*, January/February 2003.
Robert D. King	"Treason and Traitors," *Society*, January/February 1998.
Stanley Kober	"Why Spy? The Uses and Misuses of Intelligence," *USA Today*, March 1998.
Stephanie Myers	"How Safe Is Your Communication?" *Shield*, Summer/Fall 2000.
William E. Odom	"Break Up the FBI," *Wall Street Journal*, June 12, 2002.
Katherine McIntire Peters	"Lost in Translation," *Government Executive*, May 2002.
Ralph Peters	"The Black Art of Intelligence," *American Spectator*, July/August 2002.
Edward T. Pound and Brian Duffy	"The Ferrets and the Moles," *U.S. News & World Report*, September 10, 2001.
Andrew Roberts	"Bring Back 007," *Spectator*, October 6, 2001.
Jeffrey Rosen	"Security Check," *New Republic*, December 16, 2002.
David E. Rosenbaum	"When Government Doesn't Tell," *New York Times*, February 3, 2002.
Gabriel Schoenfeld	"How Inept Is the FBI?" *Commentary*, May 2002.
Jake Tapper	"The Spy Who Came in from the Mosque," *Weekly Standard*, January 13, 2003.
Charlotte Twight	"Watching You: Systematic Federal Surveillance of Ordinary Americans," *Independent Review*, Fall 1999.
J. Michael Waller	"Espionage and National Security," *Insight*, April 2, 2001.

Websites

Federation of American Scientists	*Intelligence Resource Program.* Website includes official and unofficial resources on intelligence policy, structure, function, organization, and operations. www.fas.org/irp/index.html.
Jane's Information Group	*Jane's IntelWeb.* Website includes daily intelligence bulletins on intelligence activities worldwide and access to *Jane's Intelligence Review*, a publication that examines the intelligence community, economic espionage, and aerospace security. http://intelweb.janes.com.
Political Science Department at Loyola College in Maryland	*Strategic Intelligence.* Website includes links to U.S. and international intelligence agencies and organizations that study intelligence and intelligence policy, and a substantial volume of current and historical documents, including articles, legislation, hearings, and testimony. www.loyola.edu/dept/politics/intel.html.

Index